grief
and
mourning
in cross-cultural
perspective

paul c. rosenblatt
r. patricia walsh
douglas a. jackson

HRAF Press
1976

58736

ABOUT THE AUTHORS

PAUL C. ROSENBLATT is a professor in the Department of Family Social Science and the Department of Psychology at the University of Minnesota. His previous cross-cultural work on various aspects of close social relationships has led to publication in such scholarly journals as *Ethnology, Southwestern Journal of Anthropology, Journal of Personality and Social Psychology, Developmental Psychology, Social Forces, Journal of Marriage and the Family, Journal of Comparative Family Studies, Journal of Sex Research, Omega,* and *Behavior Science Research.* Recently he has been looking at togetherness and apartness in families by doing observational and questionnaire studies and by studying diaries of U.S. pioneers.

R. PATRICIA WALSH is an assistant professor in the Psychology Department at Loyola-Marymount University in Los Angeles. She has a Ph.D. in Psychology from the University of Minnesota, and her current scholarly work deals with attitudes toward the aged.

DOUGLAS A. JACKSON has a master's degree in Family Social Science from the University of Minnesota, where, among other things, he worked on becoming a marriage counselor and family life educator. Currently he is living in southern California.

International Standard Book Number: 0-87536-333-4
Library of Congress Catalog Card Number: 76-29270

Contents

Preface

The work reported here was supported by Public Health Service Grant No. R01-MH-18453 from the National Institute of Mental Health and by the Agricultural Experiment Station of the University of Minnesota. Many people contributed to the project and the preparation of the manuscript. We are particularly indebted to the staff of the St. Paul Campus Library of the University of Minnesota for assistance in acquiring ethnographic materials. For comments on preliminary drafts of the manuscript, we are indebted to many people, particularly Michael R. Cunningham, Raoul Naroll, Richard A. Shweder, and Sandra L. Titus. For statistical advice, we are indebted to Kinley Larntz.

Acknowledgments

For permission to publish quotations, thanks are due to the following: to the Wenner-Gren Foundation for Anthropological Research, Thomas Gladwin, and Seymour B. Sarason for permission to quote from *Viking Fund Publications in Anthropology 20*, "Truk: Man in Paradise" (copyright 1954); to Frank Cass & Co., London, for permission to quote from *Niger Ibos* by George Thomas Basden; to Cambridge University Press for permission to quote from *The Andaman Islanders* by Alfred R. Radcliffe-Brown; to Random House, Inc., for permission to quote from *Jungle People* by Jules Henry; to Simon & Schuster for permission to quote from *The Forest People* by Colin M. Turnbull (copyright 1961); to the American Anthropological Association for permission to quote from "Religion of the Ifugaos," by Roy Franklin Barton, *Memoir 65:* 172, 1946; to the University of Illinois Press for permission to quote from *The Cubeo,* by Irving Goldman (copyright 1963); to The Catholic University of America Press for permission to quote from *The Gros Ventres of Montana* by Regina Flannery; to the American Anthropological Association for permission to quote from the "The Autobiography of a Papago Woman," by Ruth M. Underhill, *Memoir 46:* 50, 1936; to the University of Chicago Press for permission to quote from *Desert People* by Mervyn J. Meggitt (copyright 1965); to Cambridge University Press for permission to quote from *The Negritos of Malaya* by Ivor H. N. Evans; to Liveright Publishing Co. for permission to quote from *General Introduction to Psychoanalysis* by Sigmund Freud; to Margaret Mead for permission to quote from *Fijian Village* by Buell H. Quain;

vii

to Oxford University Press for permission to quote from *Akwe-Shavante Society* by David Maybury-Lewis (copyright 1967); to AMS Press, Inc., for permission to quote from *The Eyak* by Kaj Birket-Smith and Frederica DeLaguna; to the Humanities Press and to Anthropological Publications for permission to quote from *The Todas*, by William H. R. Rivers; to the University of Washington Press for permission to quote from *Death in Murelaga* by William A. Douglass; to Faber & Faber for permission to quote from *Baba of Karo* by Michael G. Smith; and to the University of California Press for permission to quote from "Yokuts and Western Mono Ethnography," *University of California Anthropological Records 10,* 1948, by Anna H. Gayton.

Grief and Mourning

Introduction

"My wife was sick for two months before she died. After a month she no longer heard me when I spoke to her and I knew she would die. Before she died she told me to be sure and take care of our children and I told her not to worry about it, for I would. Finally one morning at about ten o'clock she died. I cried and cried. She stayed on the mat in the house for three days and people brought all sorts of gifts, cloth and lavalavas. Then we buried her; we dug a hole in the floor of the house and buried her there. After that for three months I just stayed in the house, I above and she below the ground. Finally her mother came to me and told me I must get out and walk around, for if I just stayed there every day all day I would be sick too and would die. So I went out of the house and worked again . . . ." [Gladwin and Sarason, "Truk: Man in Paradise," 1953: 158]. [The Trukese are a people who live in the Central Caroline Islands, just north of the equator, in the Pacific.]

For people in all human societies, the death of familiar people is a constant. The ethnographic passages quoted throughout this book illustrate the fact that grief feelings are not unique to people in Western civilization. The experience of grief seems to be one of the costs of being human. The gains from long-term contact and interdependence are often followed by the agony, anger, and feelings of emptiness and sorrow that result from the death of someone who has been important to one. The following quote is a poignant illustration of the linkage of grief to interdependence.

"O my dear husband, why have you left me alone, why have you abandoned me? How happily we have passed the years together in harmony, until cruel fate and the *tunchi* of the treacherous enemy separated us! You will never again wake me in the morning with your speech, when you were cooking your tobacco water and guayusa at the fire! I shall never any more hand you the *pininga* with manioc-beer and bring you your meal. Never any more will you send me out to the fields in the morning to fetch manioc and sweet potatoes, or remind me to take care of the swine and the fowls and the hunting dogs! And when friends came to visit us, who was it that always used to call me to welcome them with nice, fresh *nihamanchi?* Who will hereafter fell the trees for me and clear the ground to make the manioc and banana plantations, or help me with cleaning and tending the fields? Who will hereafter make a red-striped *tarachi* for me for the feasts, who will bring me game from the forest or the gaily-coloured birds which you used to shoot with your blowgun and your poisoned arrows? All this you did for me, but now you lie there mute and lifeless. Your mouth has ceased speaking, your arm is paralyzed for ever. O, dear me, what will become of me?" [Karsten, *The Head Hunters of Western Amazonas*, 1935: 7, 457]. [The name of the cultural group involved is the Jivaro.]

Because grief and mourning are topics that touch the lives of all people, this book addresses the reader without specialized education in the behavioral sciences as well as the behavioral science scholar and the scholarly practitioner. A few definitions may aid the reader in understanding the book. By grief we mean the sorrow, mental distress, emotional agitation, sadness, suffering, and related feelings caused by a death. By bereavement we mean both the period of time following a death, during which grief occurs, and also the state of experiencing grief. By mourning we mean the culturally defined acts that are usually performed when a death occurs. The mourning period is the culturally defined time or typical period of time during which these acts of mourning are conventionally performed. The distinction between grief and mourning that we draw, a distinction discussed by Averill (1968) and going back in works in English at least to the first English translation of Durkheim's *The Elementary Forms of Religious Life* (1915), makes it possible to study the effect of culture on emotional behavior. However, it is, like any distinction of biology or psychology on the one hand and culture or society on the other, only of limited usefulness. All grief behavior by adults will, of course, be patterned, modified, and perhaps even coerced by culture, and any mourning act may be influenced by the biology or psychology of grief.

We have studied grief and mourning in seventy-eight cultures. These cultures vary widely in complexity, technology, and degree of contact with Western civilization and with major religious systems. This book provides the perspective on grief and mourning we obtained after careful, detailed study of ethnographic descriptions of those seventy-eight cultures. Technical details of the study are contained in the Appendix to this book. Our basic research procedure was to have two trained raters independently evaluate our seventy-eight societies on the cultural attributes of interest to us. When we wanted a measure of frequency of crying in bereavement, for example, two raters read closely the ethnographic descriptions of grief in each of the seventy-eight societies in our sample and estimated the frequency of crying by bereaved adults in each society.

A crucial issue in a study such as this one is the representativeness of the sample of cultures. If the cultures sampled are representative of all human cultures, it is more likely that generalizations from that sample to humanity in general will be valid. The standard way to establish that a sample is representative is to demonstrate that a universe of units has been defined and that cases have been drawn from that universe in a way that gives an unbiased representation of the universe. In our study, we began with a universe of 186 world culture areas (Murdock 1967, 1968; Murdock and White 1969). This universe includes a place for virtually all of the thousands of known world cultures. Each of our seventy-eight cultures comes from a different one of the 186 culture areas. We did not sample randomly. We were constrained by what was available at and through the University of Minnesota libraries; we needed societies with adequate descriptions of death customs; and we wanted to avoid using materials from culture areas containing the Aymara (Carter 1968), Mapuche (Faron 1963), LoDagaa (Goody 1962), and Kota (Mandelbaum 1959), since descriptions of these cultures had stimulated many of the hypotheses we tested. It would have been a blunder in epistemology to test hypotheses using the same evidence that stimulated them. Given our constraints, our sample is reasonably representative. If there is bias, it might be against societies in which people hide grief and mourning from ethnographers or in which grief and mourning behavior are very simple and hence seem inadequately described.

Our Aims

One aim of this book is to identify some of the needs, emotions, beliefs, and problems in social relations that are fundamentally human in reaction to a death. The book provides some indication of what is universal —or nearly so —in the species when a death of someone close to one has occurred.

A second aim of the book is to identify some of the cultural responses to the needs and problems that a death creates. How are individual and group needs met? How are the problems created by emotional reactions to a death dealt with? In our research we have hunted for cross-cultural regularities in adaptations or solutions to the problems a death creates. We have concentrated on drawing from our data answers to these questions: Assuming that anger and aggression are ordinarily components of bereavement, what are the common ways of dealing with such anger and aggression? What residues of relationship are there after someone important to one has died? What customary practices facilitate or inhibit widow remarriage? What customary practices terminate bereavement effectively?

We have also been concerned with factors influencing the choice of solutions to problems. For example why does house abandonment by a widow seem the preferred means of facilitating her remarriage in some societies; while in other societies destruction of personal property of the deceased seems the preferred means? This concern with factors influencing the choice of solutions to problems reflects our belief that solutions to problems are potential sources of new problems. Thus an awareness of factors affecting solutions may help us to understand some of the secondary problems that are created by attempts to deal with primary problems.

A third aim of this book is to understand the death customs that occur commonly in other societies. Many customs have been observed widely around the world —for example isolation of the bereaved, taboos on speaking the name of the dead, use of ritual specialists such as priests or undertakers in funeral ceremonies, and final funeral ceremonies which terminate the mourning period weeks, months, or years after a death. As a contribution to explaining the commonality of these customs, we have attempted to identify the aspects of culture and of grief and mourning to which they are linked. For example, in Chapter 2 we discuss the role of ritual specialists in the control of anger and aggression in bereavement.

A fourth and final aim of this book is to get perspective on what goes on in the United States when a death occurs. It is almost impossible to understand a single society or to get perspective on one's own society without knowing something about alternatives. For most death customs and beliefs, the standard culture of most of the inhabitants of the United States seems to be homogeneous, a single ethnographic case.

A cross-cultural perspective can provide insights that are difficult or impossible to achieve by people who are familiar with only a single culture. One takes things for granted about one's own culture or accepts cultural rationalizations as valid explanations for what is going on. Americans may, for example, accept the role of funeral directors and accept laws dealing with the property of a deceased person in a way that neither provides substantial understanding of the value of the customs nor questions whether other ways of behaving might be better or as good. Until one can compare American customs with others, as this book does, one is not in a position to understand the value and the limitations of American practice. In the process of studying grief and mourning cross-culturally, we can approach more closely to an understanding of what our basic needs are, what our cultural biases are, what we have that is worth keeping, what needs we satisfy inadequately, how we are like humans in general, and how our society is like societies in general.

A cross-cultural perspective is also necessary for epistemological reasons. How can one understand or generalize from a single case with any confidence? One cannot. There are myriad explanations of a single case. Euro-American society is to a large extent a single case. To understand it, we must look at many cases. The cross-cultural perspective of this book thus provides analyses of a power that would be impossible to achieve if we looked only at our own society.

Framework for Thinking about Grief and Mourning

In developing the conceptual framework for our work, we relied most of all on publications by Averill (1968), van Gennep

(1960), Gorer (1965), Hertz (1960), Lindemann (1944), and Mandelbaum (1959). Their work and ours can be presumed to have a foundation in common human experiences and in Western culture. In addition, their work and ours have roots in a scholarly literature in which publications by Bowlby (1961), Eliot (1948), Freud (1959), Lafitau (1724), Malinowski (1948), and Marris (1958) are among those which have had greatest impact. We present the following conceptual framework so that the reader can see some of the assumptions with which we worked and so that the reader will find it easier to place the various discussions in this book into a broader frame of reference for thinking about grief and mourning.

At the death of a person important in one's life, one generally experiences strong emotion and marked change in patterns of behavior (Averill 1968; Freud 1959; Gorer 1965; Lindemann 1944). Among these emotions may be feelings that could be labeled sadness, anger, fear, anxiety, guilt, loneliness, numbness, and general tension. The marked change in patterns of behavior frequently includes loss of appetite and consequent weight loss, disruption of work activities, loss of interest in things ordinarily interesting, a decrease in sociability, disrupted sleep, and disturbing dreams. These feelings and dispositional changes may result from many things, including uncertainty about what to do, loss of gratification, and disruption of familiar patterns of living. The problems can be expected to be greater when the death is unexpected (Gorer 1965: chap. 6) and when the uncertainty about what to do, the loss of gratification, and the disruption of familiar patterns are greater (Hertz 1960: 76; Volkart and Michael 1957).

If people who are bereaved are to return to reasonably normal patterns of productivity and social life, they need to "work through" the loss (Freud 1959; Gorer 1965; Hertz 1960: 82; Lindemann 1944). Working-through processes include acceptance of the loss, extinction of no longer adaptive behavioral dispositions, acquistion of new behavioral dispositions and relationships, and dissipation of guilt, anger, and other disruptive emotions. The working-through process is at least partly channeled and facilitated by custom (Averill 1968; van Gennep 1960: chap. 8; Goody 1962: chap. 3; Gorer 1965; Lindemann 1944; Volkart and Michael 1957).

The relation between working-through processes of individuals and behaviors required by custom are complex. It may be that in many cases custom coerces behaviors that are unneeded—for example requiring crying and self-injury of persons who if anything are relieved that the death occurred. It also may be that customs help in working-through processes for many people who, if left on their own, would not work through or would not work through so well (Gorer 1965). The customs may, in addition, channel the working-through that would go on anyhow but that would have gone on with more social friction. Where customs require emotional expression, it is often very difficult for an observer —and perhaps even for the persons expressing emotion—to judge whether in any specific case the emotions expressed are genuine. This may mean that grief coerced by custom may produce in many bereaved persons all the feelings and psychological work that generally stem from spontaneous grief.

Another thing that customs often coerce is dependence on others, on people who help with ceremonies and body disposal or who support the bereaved in various ways during the mourning period (Gorer 1965; Mandelbaum 1959). Even in the absence of customs requiring such dependent behavior, many bereaved might be dependent on others. When such customs are present, however, some bereaved may be dependent who do not need to be, and some may be dependent who need to be but who would not be in the absence of customary requirement. From another perspective, help requirements coerce those people who support the bereaved, offer sympathy, attend ceremonies, and so on. The required support serves to obligate the bereaved to those providing the support, so that there is greater chance of reciprocation when the supporters subsequently are themselves in need of help. Required support thus helps to tie people to each other (Mandelbaum 1959).

One might look at death customs as providing status passage, both for the dead and for the bereaved (van Gennep 1960: chap. 8; Hertz 1960). A dead person, over the cycle of death ceremonies, is passed from the land of the living to the land of the dead; a bereaved person is passed from the state of mourner to the state of nonmourner. The psychological processes in the

bereaved that parallel the status passages can be crudely categorized as those that move the bereaved from a state of numbness to a state of acute grief to a state of working through of
grief to a state of nonbereavement (Averill 1968; Gorer 1965:
75-83; Lindemann 1944).

In many societies, one mechanism that may work to promote
the readjustment process is the provision of a final death
ceremony some weeks, months, or years after a death (Gorer
1965: 129-30; Hertz 1960: 53-76; Mandelbaum 1959). The ceremony may provide conditions that facilitate working through
of grief and may constitute a commitment to terminate mourning. Moreover, a mourner who knows that a final ceremony
is coming may do the psychological work necessary to accept
the transition back to the state of being nonbereaved. Data
and more elaborate discussion concerning final death ceremonies are presented in Chapter 5.

From the perspective of roles, death empties roles that had
been occupied by the deceased (Forde 1962; Goody 1962; Volkart and Michael 1957). The more roles a deceased person
occupied and the more important these roles were, the more
disruptive the death will be to organizations and groups of
which the deceased was a member. Bereavement and mourning
may also, at least temporarily, empty roles occupied by the
bereaved (van Gennep 1960: chap. 8). One thing that *must* be
accomplished following a death is to refill the roles, which
requires identifying persons to occupy the roles, recruiting
them, and certifying their new positions. Certain funeral customs may provide this refilling of roles through identification,
recruitment, and certification of heirs and successors to the
deceased (and perhaps through identification of temporary
replacements for the bereaved).

From a social solidarity perspective, a death is both a loss
and a threat to group solidarity (Forde 1962; Hertz 1960: 77;
Malinowski 1948: 52-53; Mandelbaum 1959; Radcliffe-Brown
1964: 285). Social solidarity is especially important following
a death, because a death may produce such potentially disruptive dispositions as anger and unwillingness to cooperate.
To maintain social solidarity, potentially disruptive dispositions may have to be channeled in less disruptive directions
and limited in intensity. Furthermore, ceremonies following a

death may reinforce remaining ties, sort out who is in and who is not in a group, and reinforce ties through shared work and coordination required by ceremonies (Carter 1968). Eulogies, which are common around the world, may be one device for promoting solidarity. They may, by praising the dead, indirectly reward the living for their past loyalty. Then, too, eulogies may express group norms in a way that helps to recommit people to the norms (Goody 1962: 29-30). Eulogies may, for example, be a way of telling people in the group that if they follow the norms they will receive high praise at their own deaths.

Why This Study?

In the United States, there is a great and increasing demand for death education and counseling. The demand comes from many sources. These include the dissatisfaction, among some groups of people, with religious answers to existential questions, the growing infusion of behavioral sciences into religion, the publicity given to apparently irrational elements in American funerals, and the increased consumption of mental health services by people in acute problem states. Professionals who work in this area provide counseling and education, but the data base is small. One reason for this lack of data may be that many of the professionals have a particularistic orientation and training, which means that even when a professional has an interesting hunch about a specific case or about people in general, there is no inclination to do research on the dynamics or generality of the phenomenon. And since most professionals are practitioners rather than writer-scholars, neither a hunch nor the accumulated wisdom of years of practice is likely to get transmitted broadly.

Another reason for the small data base is that there are norms of propriety that prevent the systematic gathering of data from recently bereaved persons, systematic experimentation with means of dealing with a loss, or even studies requiring substantial penetration of the fronts people present when recalling bereavement experiences. These norms also contribute to the paucity of data on grief, mourning, and the means of dealing with the problems created by death. Thus, there is a great need for more knowledge in this area. Cross-cultural research, by enabling us to put American society into the perspective provided by the large mass of ethnographic descriptions available in the area of grief and mourning, can add a great deal to our understanding of grief and mourning. The approach we have taken in this work is only one of many that can and should be taken. It has its limitations (which we touch on throughout the book), but it also has yielded interesting and important ideas.

Part 1.

The Expression of Emotion

In the Introduction, we listed four aims of our work. One aim has been to identify what is fundamentally human in reactions to a death. In Chapter 1, we discuss two areas of emotionality in which we have searched for the fundamentally human: the universality of emotional expression in bereavement and the universality of sex differences in the expression of emotion during bereavement. We have asked whether it is fundamentally human to express emotion following a death and whether it is fundamentally human for the sexes to be emotional in different ways or in different amounts.

Our second aim for this book has been to identify the cultural responses to the needs and problems a death creates. In Chapter 2, we focus on the cultural response to one problem, the problem of controlling the anger and aggression that might occur during bereavement. We believe that the anger and aggression of bereavement are potentially of danger to ongoing social relationships in a society. We have, therefore, sought to identify the common cultural responses to such anger and aggression, to try to understand the factors influencing the choice of cultural responses, and to document the consequences of inadequate control of anger and aggression in bereavement.

Our third aim has been to try to understand common death customs. In the discussions in Chapter 2 of the control of anger and aggression, we attempt to provide some understanding of three cross-culturally common death customs: the marking of the bereaved, the isolation of the bereaved, and the use of ritual specialists, such as priests, in the period immediately after the occurrence of a death.

A fourth aim of this book has been to get perspective on grief and mourning in the United States. In the two chapters in this section of the book we provide perspective on several issues that are of concern in America: the extent to which overt expression of grief is natural or unnatural, the meaning of sex difference (or lack of difference) in emotionality during bereavement, and the uses of ritual specialists, such as funeral directors.

Chapter 1.

The Expression of Emotion in Bereavement

It is when the moment of death arrives that the tumult begins. There is an outburst of wailing, the women particularly giving full vent to their grief. Sometimes a wife or mother will rush from the hut heedless of direction, waving her arms, and beating her breast as she bewails her loss at the top of her voice. Such an one will wander aimlessly for hours, crying the same words, until she becomes an automaton. Eventually, after possibly being out all night, she struggles back to her hut, physically and mentally exhausted. This is not, however, the common practice. Usually, the stricken woman is surrounded by her friends and induced or, failing that, forced to sit down. This is done to safeguard her, for often a woman, bereaved of husband or child, will work herself into a state of frenzy and she cannot be trusted to go forth alone lest she do injury to herself, or even commit suicide. . . . For a time, there is great confusion and noise, all wailing in unison, and then the casual visitors withdraw, leaving the family to mourn their loss undisturbed [Basden, *Niger Ibos*, 1966b: 270].

Are Other People Like Americans?

If we are going to assert that it is valid to compare society with society and American society with others, it is important that we establish at the onset that grief in other societies resembles grief in America. If we are going to use information from societies like Truk and the Jivaro, as we did in the quoted ethnographic passages in the Introduction, to tell the reader something about human bereavement and to place American grief and mourning in perspective, we must establish that there is adequate cross-cultural similarity. If people in other cultures typically react to a death without the sorrow and other emotions common to bereaved Americans, an analysis of the death customs of these other cultures may have little relevance to grief and mourning in America.

A basic presupposition throughout our research has been that people everywhere build long-term, interdependent relations. We assume further that these relationships produce feelings of attachment and caring, and that the termination of these relationships produces considerable distress and personal disorganization. Hence we would expect that deaths would produce signs of emotional distress for some people in any society. Although the dynamics of emotion and emotional suppression in societies very different from our own have not been studied in detail, we conjecture that there is enough similarity in human relations and human emotionality around the world that in virtually any society deaths would typically produce signs of emotional distress in some people.

To establish that similarities exist, we present in the first section of this chapter data on the expression of emotion in bereavement. Unfortunately, the gap between what we would like to investigate in the area of emotional expression and what the ethnographic literature allows us to investigate is enormous. It is impossible to study cross-culturally the fine grain of emotional behavior, to probe for similarities and differences in most of the behaviors that have been described in the literature on grief in the United States—depression, somatic symptoms, anxiety, disruption of eating, feelings of disorientation, and so on. Even if the behaviors were mentioned in various ethnographies, we would still have problems if we lacked data on frequency, duration, and variations in occurrence correlated with type of death and with the relationship of the bereaved to the deceased. Even if the behaviors were described, it would still be necessary to have data on how these behaviors are defined and understood by the people in each society. But these data are also lacking. Thus, we are only able to trace cross-cultural similarities in extremely crude outline. We can with such crudeness establish whether people in the

United States are, on a few key aspects of emotion, similar to or quite different from people in other societies and if there is little or enormous variability cross-culturally. But we cannot, with the data now available, get beyond the crude outline to the subtleties that must eventually be studied for thorough understanding of grief in the United States and in the species.

Crying

In the cross-cultural literature that we used, crying is the best-described type of emotional behavior of bereaved persons. In our data, crying was rated as present for some bereaved persons in seventy-two of seventy-three societies; five societies were not ratable because of inadequate or contradictory information. Of the seventy-three societies that could be rated on crying, only the Balinese appeared to lack crying in bereavement.

The reader who is interested in the formal measurement and statistics underlying our work should turn to the Appendix of this book. Throughout the book, our ratings deal with deaths of adults and behavior of survivors who are typical adults in their society, as opposed to such people as royalty, slaves, and religious specialists. Of course our ratings are not infallible; there may have been errors in the literature we used, our raters may have made errors, and errors may have occurred in the statistical processing of the ratings. But it seems from our data on crying that, as in our society, crying is a part of bereavement for some people in most societies.

Two of the raters on our project attempted to evaluate frequency of crying in bereavement. The ratings were made on a five-point scale ranging from crying "absent" to crying "very frequent." Sixty-nine of the seventy-eight societies in our sample could be rated by both raters. Sixty-seven of the sixty-nine societies were rated by both raters as having at least frequent crying at death, and fifty-six of these had the highest rating possible—a rating of "very frequent" by both raters. Only the Balinese, with a rating of "absent," and their near neighbors, the Javanese, with a rating equivalent to "crying rarely present," deviated from the worldwide pattern. The fact that the Javanese are similar to the geographically close and culturally related Balinese increases the chances that there is really something to explain about the Balinese, that our ratings of Balinese crying are not measurement errors.

Puzzled about the Balinese, one of us (PCR) learned rudimentary Bahasa Indonesia and spent twenty-four days in Bali trying to comprehend Balinese emotionality. A proper study would take quite a long time, but here are some impressions. Emotional behavior in Bali seems 98 percent of the time to be what would seem perfectly appropriate for Americans. Crying in Bali may be odd, however. Many children and two adult women were observed making crying noises, but they did not appear to be producing tears. Furthermore, in the case of the two women and in the case of most of the children, crying ended more abruptly than crying with tear production does in the United States. Perhaps crying with tears is harder to stop than crying without tears. Although a long-term study would allow for much more confident evaluation of the Balinese situation, it is possible that the Balinese simply do not often produce tears. If so, their lack of crying when bereaved is not discrepant from their emotional behavior in other situations where some Americans might cry. If Balinese crying is rare, even in small children, the temptation is to offer a physical (genetic, dietary, climatic) explanation. However, the Balinese have religious beliefs that encourage people to be calm and undisturbed. These beliefs may also be a factor in controlling tear production. One possible symptom of such control is that three different men, while telling about very unpleasant things that had happened to them (e.g. the death of three of one man's children), smiled or laughed during the telling, a smile or laugh that seemed to say: "If I don't do this, I must cry." Such smiling and laughter occurs also in the United States, but it seems a more common pattern in Bali.

Two Balinese men volunteered information about grief and mourning. Both said that people do cry at a death, particularly if a parent dies. At the only funeral PCR attended in Bali, there was ample crying with tears, but the deceased and all the bereaved were recent Chinese immigrants to Bali or their offspring. Although they had adopted many local customs, their funeral practices seemed quite Chinese, following, for example, mourning dress patterns that have been described for the Chinese in general (Wolf 1970). So there is every reason to believe that the emotionality in grief of the Chinese of Bali was atypical of Bali.

In sum, the crying data from our sample of societies seem to indicate a degree of similarity among the people of various cultures in the extent to which a death causes an emotional reaction and a degree of similarity between people in other societies and people in the United States in emotional reaction to a death. These similarities, as well as elements of uniqueness, can perhaps be more pointedly illustrated by the quotes dealing with the Trukese and the Jivaro in the Introduction, the passage dealing with the Ibo at the beginning of this chapter, and the following paragraphs dealing with the Thonga, the Andamanese, and the Aweikoma. Following burial and a prayer:

> The wailing begins. The women get on their feet and shout loudly, throwing themselves on the ground. The wife of the deceased cries more than any one else: "I have remained alone in the lonely plain. . . . Where did you go? You have left me." The wailing generally starts on a very high note and finishes a little lower, expressing the pain of the heart in a touching, penetrating manner. Here is one of these sentences which can hardly be called a song. I heard it in 1893 at the burial of a young woman who was found drowned in the lake of Rikatla.
>
> "O my mother! O my mother! You have left me, where did you go?!"
>
> The parents-in-law lament over their daughter, the new widow. Everybody then begins to lament over his own relatives who have died recently [Junod, *The Life of a South African Tribe*, 1927: *1*, 143]. [The group described is the Thonga.]

> The relatives sit around the corpse weeping at intervals, while some of the men take it in turn to sing songs during the hours of darkness. This, so they say, is to keep away the spirits that have caused the death, and so prevent them from further mischief. When a man or woman dies in the prime of life after a short illness the friends and relatives often break out in anger which they express in different ways. A man will shout threats and curses at the spirits that he conceives to be responsible for the death of his friend. He may pick up his bow and discharge his arrows in all directions, or in some other way give expression to his angry feelings [Radcliffe-Brown, *The Andaman Islanders*, 1964: 110]. [The Andaman Islands lie between Burma and Sumatra.]

When I climbed into my hammock that night, there had

been a lull in the weeping, but I was awakened several hours before dawn by the frantic keening of Waikome. One by one, others joined her, and I knew then that the baby was dead. As I watched, the emotion gradually grew more intense; and some went to join the group mourning around the child. There was no play-acting here, no singling out of those whom relationship obliged to weep from those who could just look on. Those who were not affected kept aloof and performed their daily tasks, but those who felt an identification with the bereaved parents mourned with them. Ndili's second cousin sat with his arm around him and wept, but Ndili's brother seemed entirely untouched and soon went off to get honey. At last, late in the morning, the parents took up their little bundle and went away, and the sound of their keening came back to us through the forest.

That day no one went hunting even though there was no meat in camp. Toward noon Waipo said to me, his voice intense with fear: "You'd better pack your things, because we're going away from here right away. We thought we would stay and kill another tapir, but the baby died; and now we have to move." Who knows what might have happened if they had remained? The ghost-soul of the baby might have taken someone along with it or the ghost-soul which had killed it might kill again. . . .

If we think of death among ourselves and the demonstrations that accompany it among the less inhibited members of our own society, if we disregard for a moment the wild surroundings, the rhythmic keening, the fear of the ghost-soul, and even, perhaps, the useless medicine that was forced between the choking child's lips (although, Heaven knows, that too might easily be duplicated in our society), we cannot but see a striking resemblance between the grief of Waikome and Ndili and the members of their group and similar displays in our own society. Among ourselves, anger is generally thrust into the background and often disappears entirely when grief is sincere, but among the Kaingang it pervades the entire scene and manifests itself in an irritability that may easily become anger [Henry, *Jungle People*, 1964: 66]. [A description of the Aweikoma (Kaingang) of southern Brazil.]

Anger and Aggression

As the preceding quotations dealing with the Andamanese and the Aweikoma suggest, anger and aggression may be part of grief and mourning for many non-Western peoples. (See Chapter 2 for documentation of the anger and aggression of bereavement in the United States.) In our sample of societies, anger and aggression were judged present in fifty (76 percent) of sixty-six societies that were ratable on at least one of nineteen measures we made of anger and aggression. It is possible that anger is present but hidden in the modal bereaved person in the sixteen societies that seemed to lack anger and aggression in bereavement. After all, it has been known for quite some time that many bereaved people in the United States conceal anger (Lindemann 1944). But at this point the cross-cultural data on anger and aggression allow us only to make the limp statement that anger and aggression occur during bereavement in many societies.

We were able to measure separately self-directed anger-aggression and anger-aggression directed away from self. One might argue that both self-directed and other-directed anger-aggression stem from the same internal states or affect each other and that as a consequence the two categories of anger-aggression should be associated. Alternatively, one could argue that the two kinds of anger-aggression represent different and more or less mutually exclusive processes, so that the more anger and aggression are directed in one direction, the less they are directed in the other. Other-directed anger could, for example, be a self-protective displacement of anger toward self onto targets other than self. But in fact, in our data, self-directed and other-directed anger and aggression are associated. The more there is of one, the more there is of the other. Either both kinds of anger and aggression arise from the same sources or there are causal relations between the two types of anger and aggression. For example hurting oneself may motivate one to attack others who have not hurt themselves, or attacking others may motivate one, through guilt feelings, to hurt oneself. The following passage from an ethnography dealing with the Mbuti Pygmies of the Congo may help to make the fact of relationship of the two kinds of anger-aggression less abstract.

There was a finality and terrible emptiness in old Baleki-mito's death which could not be answered, for which there was no explanation, not even through sorcery or witchcraft. For the moment it seemed that the Pygmies, faced with the death of an old and well-loved and respected person such as this old lady, had nothing to cling to, and I was genuinely afraid that some of them would come to harm. Young and old alike crowded around the house, trying to force their way to Balekimito's deathbed. They were even fighting to get in, and once inside they fought to get out. At one point several children came flying out in a frenzy and threw themselves onto the ground, beating it with their arms and legs, kicking and biting at anyone who tried to comfort them. Inside, the commotion was even worse—Asofalinda, looking almost as old as her dead mother, had put a noose around her neck and seemed to be trying to strangle herself, full of remorse at having let her mother die. It took three men to take the noose from her neck, and when they finally tore it from her she ran outside and collapsed on the ground, sobbing her heart out. . . .

[Masisi] stalked out of the veranda and down to the far end of the little village, brandishing one hand above his head, telling everyone to stop making such a dreadful noise, that it was not doing any good to anybody. "Crying is a matter of the immediate family," he said. "She was a mother to us all, but for all of us to cry is just too much noise." He clutched his head to illustrate the point, then grabbed a couple of children, one of them his own, and sent them flying. By now his temper was no longer artificial, and the women decided it was wiser to keep out of his way, and left [Turnbull, *The Forest People*, 1961: 49-51]. [The Mbuti Pygmies live in the Ituri Forest of the Congo.]

Fear

Fear has not been well documented in the literature on grief in the United States. Yet our own experiences in bereavement and our unsystematic observations of others in bereavement suggest that fear may be very common—fear of a corpse, fear of being alone, fear of one's own death, fear of not behaving properly, fear of insanity, fear of being unable to have the needs satisfied that the deceased person had satisfied, fear of behaving in public with excessive grief, fear of what one's irritability may do to one's relations with others, and so on. In the ethnographic material we used, only fear of bodies and fear of ghosts were measurable, and at that they were only measurable on a very coarse grain. We found fear of corpses to be present in eight (38 percent) of twenty-one measurable societies and ghost fear to be present in thirty-seven (84 percent) of forty-four measurable societies. Altogether, some kind of fear was present in thirty-eight (76 percent) of fifty societies for which we have at least one fear measure. It may be that the English-language category labeled "fear" lumps together what most other languages would place in distinct categories, but if it is granted that it makes sense to talk about fear in general, then our data on fear allow us to make a limp statement similar to the one we made about anger and aggression. As is the case with anger and aggression, fear is an emotion that people may conceal; fear may actually be present in the twelve societies that seem to lack fear. But all we can really say is that fear is an emotion of bereavement in many societies.

Perspective on Emotionality

Seventy-seven of the seventy-eight societies in our sample could be measured on at least one emotionality variable. Only the Masai were unmeasurable. For all but one of the seventy-seven that could be measured on at least one variable, some kind of emotionality was judged to be present for at least some bereaved persons. The one exceptional case was the Balinese. What can we conclude about the species?

It seems basically human for emotions to be expressed in bereavement. When a person reacts with crying, overt anger, or overt fear, that person is behaving as some people in most societies do. Indeed, in the majority of societies, crying occurs frequently among people who are bereaved. At least in dim outline, American emotional responses to death seem to be like those of people in most other cultures. And at least in dim outline, the emotional responses of people in almost any culture resemble those of people in almost any other. Thus, given the weakness of the best data available, it seems not unacceptable to evaluate American society from the perspective of other societies or to assume that close social relationships produce comparable involvements in most societies.

Sex Differences in Emotionality

It is commonly assumed that the sexes differ in emotionality in many situations, including bereavement (see Bindra 1972; Glick, Weiss, and Parkes 1974: 263-65; Marris 1974: 33; and Romm 1970 for some relevant data and theory). Men appear to cry less in bereavement and to be generally less expressive of emotion (Clayton, Desmarais, and Winokur 1968; Glick, Weiss, and Parkes 1974: 263-65; Marris 1974: 33). Perhaps men in the United States experience less emotion, or perhaps they experience quite a bit of emotion that does not get expressed. Sex differences in emotion during bereavement in the United States are, to the best of our knowledge, poorly documented. Whatever the differences actually are, it is important to get a worldwide perspective on sex differences in bereavement. Is there a species-characteristic pattern, or are patterns of sex difference idiosyncratically variable? To answer the question, we evaluated, in our sample of seventy-eight societies, the aspects of sex differences that we could measure in crying, in attempted and actual self-mutilation, and in anger and aggression directed away from self.

Crying

We measured frequency of crying separately for men and for women. For sixty societies, both sexes could be rated. In thirty-two of the societies, the sexes were judged to have equal crying frequency; in twenty-eight, they were not. In all twenty-eight of the societies in which crying frequency was unequal, adult females had a greater frequency of crying than adult males. The raters also made a more sensitive, comparative measure, a single rating on each society of whether the sexes were equal or unequal in crying frequency. That rating could be made on fifty-eight of the seventy-eight societies in the sample. On that measure, women appeared to the raters to average much more crying behavior than men. The crying data indicate two things. First, in societies with a sex difference in crying, women cry more than men. Second, in many societies there is no sex inequality in crying. The paragraph at the beginning of this chapter dealing with the Ibo and the following three ethnographic quotations may help to make more vivid some of the sex differences we are discussing.

> For 10 days after the funeral, the spouse of the deceased lay on mats, covered with furs with his face against the ground. He or she did not speak or answer except to say *cway* . . . to those who came to visit them, did not warm himself even in winter, ate cold food, did not go to feasts, and went out only at night for necessities. During this time, a handful of hair

was cut from the back of the head. . . . The women wailed, especially in the morning just before daybreak, for entire weeks. Widows, in addition to this wailing, did not adorn themselves or bathe or anoint themselves, had dishevelled hair, and observed a sullen silence. . . .

This period was followed by a year of lesser mourning. . . . When a woman was in mourning, she did not visit anyone, walked with head and eyes lowered, was ill-clad and ill-combed, and had a dirty face, sometimes further blackened with charcoal. . . .

The women, especially, frequently went to mourn at the tombs of the dead outside the village. . . . [Tooker, "An Ethnography of the Huron Indians, 1615-1649," 1964: 133].

A female relative, on first arriving at the death chair, will always wail, usually with her blanket over her head, and this wailing will probably be joined in by the other female relatives that are present. Sometimes the women scratch their faces so that they run with blood and bystanders interfere and tell them, "Stop it! It does no good—even if you should kill yourself, he (she) will not come back." Men do not wail, but they sometimes chop their heads or slash their bodies with bolos, especially if it be a child of theirs who has died. [Barton, "The Religion of the Ifugaos," 1946: 172]. [The Ifugaos live in the Philippines.]

Whoever goes to the mourning must show proper grief in his attire.

This does not apply so much to the men, but the women who go to mourn must wear a simple girdle of *bingba* grass or of a string of vegetable fibres from the sweet potato, without ornaments and with very few leaves which in practice cover hardly anything. They tear their hair, sprinkle ashes over their head and body, and paint their face and all their body with juice of the *Cycnium camporum* (*mbiongo-dekurugbo*), which gives them an almost inhuman and revolting appearance. Of the women present, some go into the hut and stand near the corpse to wail and sing, others stand near the door.

The men glance inside where the body is and then squat down under the granaries or in the shade of some tree to talk about what is happening [Gero, *Death among the Azande of the Sudan*, 1968: 26].

Self-Mutilation

In the preceding two passages, those dealing with the Ifugao and the Azande, there seems to be more self-mutilation by fe-

males than by males. How general is this pattern cross-culturally? For thirty-two societies, measures of frequency of *attempted*
self-injury could be made for both men and women. In eighteen
of these thirty-two societies, the sexes were rated as equal. In
twelve of the remaining fourteen societies (including the Ifugao
and the Azande), women were rated as having a higher frequency of self-injury attempts.

For thirty-one societies, measures of frequency of *actual* self-
injury could be made for both men and women. In twenty of
these thirty-one cases, the sexes were rated as equal. In nine of
the remaining eleven cases (including the Ifugao and Azande),
women were rated as having greater frequency of actual self-
injury. Although the pattern of sex difference for self-injury
is not as strong as it is for crying, it appears that there is similarity between the two patterns. There is a great deal of sex
equality in attempted and actual self-injury cross-culturally,
but where there is not any sex equality, women tend to be
more expressive than men.

Anger and Aggression

A comparative measure of differences between men and women in anger and aggression directed at people and things
other than self could be made on thirteen societies. Although
the number of ratable cases was small, the effect was strong. Of
the thirteen societies, one was judged by both raters to have
sex equality in anger and aggression. Three were judged by one
rater to be equal and by the other rater to have more male than
female anger and aggression; the remaining nine were judged
by both raters to have more frequent male anger and aggression directed away from self.

Reflections on the Sex Differences in Emotionality

Although there is a substantial amount of similarity between
men and women in emotionality during bereavement, there
is consistency across cultures in the pattern of sex differences.
Where there are differences, women seem to cry, to attempt
self-mutilation, and actually to self-mutilate more than men;
men seem to show more anger and aggression directed away
from self.

One issue to which the data are relevant is the question of whether European and American men who cry relatively little and seem to be relatively unemotional in bereavement are suffering from some pathology. The issue is, of course, complicated, and individuals vary widely in what underlies a given pattern of emotional expression. But the cross-cultural data suggest that there is nothing particularly odd about men crying less. Men in many societies cry less. Perhaps men in general have stronger dispositions to hold back tears or not to cry, or perhaps they actually experience losses less strongly on the average. This latter possibility, implied in the work of Averill (1968) and Marris (1958, 1974), may mean that women tend to have greater attachments than men. Women, through the roles they generally occupy as mothers and wives, may develop stronger attachments on the average than men. Then, when a child or a spouse dies, it may be ordinarily experienced as a greater loss by a woman than by a man. There are, however, in addition to this attachment explanation of the sex differences in emotion in bereavement, four other explanations we think worthy of attention.

Socialization of the sexes for aggression. Crying may represent aggression (Greenacre 1966; Löfgren 1966). Thus, the sex difference in crying may stem in part from socialization of women to cry rather than to attack when frustrated. It may be that it is easier to socialize women to be nonaggressive than to socialize males (see Whiting and Edwards 1973 for cross-cultural data on childhood sex differences and similarities in aggression). It may be that traditional female roles (e.g. child care) can be carried out better if one is socialized to be less attacking; whereas traditional male roles (e.g. participation in warfare and local politics) may even be facilitated by a certain amount of willingness to be overtly angry and aggressive. Then, too, sex differences in socialization for anger and aggression may arise from the relations between the sexes. It is a well-established fact that males cross-culturally have higher public status and greater access to desirable goods and services (Rosenblatt and Cunningham n.d.). It is quite possible that an important element in this sex differentiated pattern is a male capacity to win physical battles with females (Rosenblatt and Cunningham n.d.). If fighting or the threat of it is important in main-

taining a pattern of male privilege, it may be that a socialization of females to cry or self-mutilate when angry is one
element that maintains the system or that protects women,
men, and heterosexual relationships from the deleterious consequences of high frequency of physical fighting.

Sex differences in help-seeking. Another possible explanation
of the sex differences in emotion in bereavement is that the
pattern represents different needs for help or different ways
of acquiring help. Crying has often been identified as help-
seeking behavior (Becker 1933; Bowlby 1961; Gorer 1965: 151).
Perhaps women tend to cry more because they are more in
need of help when someone dies. They may, for example, as
a result of their forced social subordination to males, be more
dependent than males for assistance and direction, so that
when someone dies they may experience a greater need for
assistance. Or perhaps the sexes do not differ in dependency,
but it is just that males, in the typical social system, can be
more direct about seeking help, while females must more
often rely on some form of indirection, such as crying.

Status and bereavement. Another possible explanation is suggested by two facts. (1) In many societies there are women who
cry and self-mutilate when a death occurs who are not close to
the deceased and who seem to be crying and self-mutilating
because it is proper for women to behave that way. (2) Women
often seem to be more coerced than men by normative requirements of extreme and long-term mourning behavior. These
two facts suggest that the sex difference in crying and self-
mutilation may actually represent cross-cultural sex differences
in status.

Women may be more coerced than men to engage in crying
and self-mutilation. When people feel that somebody should
show extreme distress, women, because of their lower status
(Rosenblatt and Cunningham n.d.), may be the ones who typically are pressed to show the greater distress. Women may
thus be used by males as either emotion-expressing or respect-
expressing surrogates. The apparent sex differences in crying
and self-mutilation may represent the same processes that
give men the right to eat first, to be the ones to drink alcohol

when alcohol is scarce, and to ride when there is only one beast of burden available for an excursion. In short, women may not experience a death more strongly; they may only be used (and allow themselves to be used) as the persons who symbolize publicly, in burdensome or self-injuring ways, the loss that all have experienced.

Alternatively, both sexes may be required to reflect their relative status by demonstrating more (if female) or less (if male) personal distress when a death occurs. It may be that it would be out of character for the high status person to self-mutilate and to cry a great deal, whereas it may be out of character for the lower status persons, the females, to be normally self-indulgent in the face of a loss. If the analysis of relative status factors is correct, we would also expect that higher status males within a society would be less expressive of grief than the lower status ones and that higher status females within a society would be less expressive of grief than lower status ones.

Politics and bereavement. The sex difference in anger and aggression not self-directed is based on only thirteen societies. We are understandably reluctant to draw strong conclusions from these data about a species pattern of anger and aggression in bereavement. Although men are significantly more likely in the thirteen societies to be overtly angry and aggressive at a target other than self, interpretation of the data is difficult. In some cases, the difference may rest on a pattern of intergroup aggression, which makes loss and revenge a normal pattern of warfare; attacks in such cases may represent politics as usual, not emotion in bereavement. In some cases, male attacks and anger may rest heavily on the encouragement and instigation of women; thus attacks directed by males against others may actually be more representative in some cases of the grief of women than of the grief of men.

Chapter Summary

In this chapter we have established that there is some similarity among societies in several of the types of emotions expressed in bereavement and that these emotional expressions are not unlike emotional expressions of Americans. We then established that cross-culturally, despite a great deal of male-female similarity, where there are sex differences in emotions in bereavement, women tend to cry and self-mutilate more, and men tend to direct anger and aggression away from self.

We have discussed the possible factors that underlie the sex differences in emotional expression, but we lack the kinds of data that would enable us to choose among explanations.

Chapter 2

The Control of Anger and Aggression

The old woman, truly grief-stricken, had embraced her dead husband's body in the hammock and rocked over it, moaning and wailing. She withdrew, however, when the younger brother of [the old man] arrived. He felt for the heartbeat and then covered the old man's face with some rags that had been the sick man's blanket. The women had all gathered to one side of the hammock and they wept continuously, chorusing the loud and emphatic wailing of the widow. The brother fetched his shotgun, moving slowly and grimly. He loaded it with a wad and turned to face the corpse. Each man now went with the same slow deliberateness to fetch his gun. The armed men formed a tight circle around the hammock, the widow in their midst pressed against it. Brandishing the weapon, the brother began the funeral declamation, a statement of grief and then anger and the threat of retaliation against the enemy. Each male mourner delivered his own address, always declaring his kinship relationship to the old man. The women accompanied the hoarse shouts of masculine anger with their own counterpoint of grief. After the last man had spoken they all fired their guns into the air together. The widow then withdrew to her hammock and lay silently while the men gathered about the hammock, caressed the corpse, and wept, accompanied in their grief by the women [Goldman, *The Cubeo Indians of the Northwest Amazon*, 1963: 185-86].

People commonly feel anger when someone close to them or important to them dies (Averill 1968; Bowlby 1961; Freud 1959; Glick, Weiss and Parkes 1974; Hertz 1960: 77; Hobson 1964; Kennell, Slyter, and Klaus 1970; Kubler-Ross 1969: 177; Lindemann 1944; Parkes 1970, 1972; Vernon 1970: 144). In theory, anger and aggression are to be expected whenever frustration occurs (Dollard et al. 1939; Freud 1959). Frustration may be defined as the blocking or delay of any goal-directed activity or as deprivation of some source of gratification. By this definition, the death of someone close or important to an individual is frustrating. In theory, and apparently in fact, such frustration disposes one to anger and aggression.

Consider a child in the United States who has just lost a great-grandparent. The child will lose the approval, interest, presents, and the anticipation of approval, interest, and presents that the great-grandparent provided. The child may lose hoped-for information about the past from the great-grandparent. The child will lose a listener and a person whose current and anticipated future behavior he can talk about. If the child obtains gratification from the longevity of kin, the loss of future increments in longevity of the great-grandparent will also be frustrating. If the child likes stability and the feeling that nothing changes except that children grow up, there will be another loss at the death of the great-grandparent. If the child likes a predictable world, the abrupt shift that occurs with the death may also be a frustration. The relationship of great-grandparent and great-grandchild may ordinarily be unimportant and not, for a child, a significant source of rewards. Yet even in this example, it seems clear that there are reasons for the child to feel anger due to frustation. The death of a spouse, lover, parent, child, significant colleague, or close friend would obviously entail much greater frustration and, presumably, anger. In these cases, one loses much more of many of the things a child loses at the death of a great-grandparent. And one loses an enormous range of other things as well. Perhaps most importantly, as Marris (1974: 21) puts it, the "thread of continuity in the interpretation of life becomes attenuated or altogether lost."

The following ethnographic passage provides a pointed illustration of anger and aggression in bereavement of a widow. The passage is useful not only as an illustration of anger and aggression but also as a reminder that people may not be aware of all the sources of their feelings of anger when a death occurs.

> When the procession arrived at the cemetery the coffin was placed next to the grave and the lid was placed on the coffin

but not nailed. The mother resumed her weeping. Each pall-bearer in turn put a dollar bill on the coffin. There was a pause and the people assembled sat around quietly. There were about a hundred in all. They were waiting for the arrival of K's daughter, a young married woman who had been delayed in getting from Rongrong, where she lived. Finally she arrived with a small party. She was met by K's wife, her own mother, who talked angrily to her, snapped at her with her handkerchief, and tried to strike her. The daughter wailed and fell to the ground and her mother broke out into loud weeping. Two men picked up the daughter and half-carried her to the coffin, at the same time protecting her from her angry and weeping mother. The lid was then nailed on the coffin and the body lowered into the grave. . . .

K's wife's anger at her daughter and her attempt to strike the latter illustrate a time when overt aggression is permitted and expected. I was told that relatives arriving late at a funeral are always thus greeted, even if they hurried as fast as they could. The survivors of the dead man's own household are angry with relatives coming from afar because they were not there when he died, and because they had not spent more time with the deceased before his death [Spoehr, "Majuro," 1949: 217-18]. [Majuro is a community in the Marshall Islands in the Pacific.]

Berkowitz (1962) has argued that cues to aggression are necessary for aggression to occur, that one must perceive reminders of aggression—such as weapons or other people aggressing—in order to aggress. However, in societies where overt anger, insults, blaming, and other attacks are common, cues to aggression are probably present much of the time in the ecology of most bereaved people. Even in societies where such cues are not commonly present, they probably exist. If so, the possibility of aggression may be present in all societies. If it can be assumed that frustration and the possibility of aggression are present early in bereavement in all societies, questions arise about the means to prevent the anger and aggression from damaging the social relations of the survivors.

Mechanisms of Aggression Control

Let us assume that anger and aggression are potential problems for any society. In any society, they could lead to injury to ingroup members and to attacks, insults, quarrels, accusations, or feuds disruptive of important social relations. It seems to us that societies faced with the potential anger and aggression of bereavement have two adaptive options: (1) to suppress anger and aggression or (2) to channel anger and aggression along nondestructive paths.

Ritual Specialists

It seems to us that if anger and aggression are to be suppressed, a societal mechanism of suppression is necessary. Strong socialization for the suppression of disruptive anger and aggression is probably not a feasible alternative, because not all persons can be trusted to have been sufficiently socialized, and because such self-suppression can lead to severe, prolonged depression. The following passage, dealing with the premodern Omaha Indians, illustrates the possible linkage between self-suppression of anger or aggression and depression.

> Mourners seem to have found relief from the mental pain of sorrow by inflicting physical pain —slashing their arms and legs. To cut locks of hair and throw them on the body was a customary expression of grief, as was wailing. At times the cries of mourners could be heard on the hills in the early morning and during the night watches. Sad as was the sound of this active expression of grief, it was not so pathetic as the silent forms of sorrow, which sometimes terminated in death. The mourner would draw his blanket over his head and with fixed downward gaze sit motionless, refusing to eat or to speak, deaf to all words of comfort and sympathy, until at last he fell senseless [Fletcher and LaFlesche, "The Omaha Tribe," 1911: 591].

The mechanisms of depression are undoubtedly varied and complex, but one possible explanation is that attempts to suppress anger and aggression through inner self-control contribute to depression. That may be one reason why societal rather than self-control mechanisms are necessary if suppression of anger and aggression is to occur. Societal mechanisms are, we think, more likely to maintain behavior. Self-control mechanisms may suppress all behaviors or may compound the problem of dependency in bereavement by increasing even further the individual's reliance on others for impetus (Ferster 1973).

The threat of retaliation does not seem to us to be a practicable means of suppressing anger and aggression. If anything, it may give some mourners an excuse to attack others. An attack on an already irritable person may, of course, motivate that person to relatively great retaliatory anger and aggression.

There are psychologists and psychiatrists who argue that suppression of anger and aggression following a frustration is impossible. We think, however, that it is important to distinguish anger and aggression stemming from recurrent frustration, such as may accumulate during prolonged coresidence with a frustrater (Bach and Wyden 1968), from the anger and aggression caused by the frustration of a death. In the former case, feelings can accumulate in a way that may make suppression, at some point, impossible. Moreover, suppression may contribute to the frustration by blinding the frustrater to one's frustration, thereby leaving the frustrater free to continue frustrating. In the case of frustration stemming from a death, however, it is ordinarily considered legitimate to express feelings in some way (see the preceding chapter). In fact, societies are generally organized to help the bereaved cope with the frustrations of a death (see Chapters 4 and 5), so that frustration is not so likely to accumulate and so that there is less point to communicating feelings of anger. Hence, we think a societal mechanism of suppression of anger and aggression in bereavement could work effectively.

In accomplishing this suppression, a societal mechanism could either (1) minimize instigations to aggression (through minimizing additional frustration or through satisfying needs created or frustrated as the result of the death) or (2) promote responses inconsistent with the expression of anger and aggression (e.g. keeping busy with funeral preparations). Ritual specialists (and the ritual they provide) seem to be optimal societal inventions for suppressing anger and aggression in these ways. We define a ritual specialist as a person with a publicly recognized role who performs predictable behaviors and guides others to perform predictable behaviors at life cycle, calendrical, political, affliction, or other ceremonies. Ritual specialization is so common cross-culturally that it seems likely that many cultures could put ritual specialization to use in suppression of the anger and aggression of bereavement if it were of use in such suppression. It seems quite feasible that once ritual specialization has been established, specialists could, with the force of recognized authority and mastery, minimize instigations to anger and aggression and promote competing responses.

Minimizing Instigations to Anger and Aggression

Ritual specialists may minimize instigations to anger and aggression through the satisfaction of dependency needs and through the provision of predictable, normatively correct things to do which minimize the frustration of not having things to do when one feels like doing something, not knowing what to do, or not knowing what will happen next. For a person who has lost somebody close, one source of feelings of grief is the loss of the one who satisfied the needs to be supported, aided, cared for, and directed, and to have something to do. These needs may be even greater during bereavement, because the bereaved may feel unsure of what to do (Habenstein 1968), have increased needs for reassurance, need help in coping with mourning norms, and have decreased motivation to initiate any activity (Lindemann 1944), including food preparation and self-care. Moreover, there may be, in bereavement, greater dependence needs due to destruction, abandonment, giving away, or putting aside of property. Such loss of property is customary in some societies (see Chapter 4) and often deprives the bereaved of useful objects or even of a dwelling. Ritual specialists may help to reduce frustration of the bereaved, satisfying these dependence needs by providing advice, instruction, assistance, and encouragement and also by instigating behavior.

The ritual activity provided by such specialists may also minimize frustration, because it is predictable and normatively correct. When bereavement pushes one to the edge of an angry explosion, any increment in frustration may produce a large magnitude of attack. To the extent that frustrations are avoided by predictable, normatively correct ritualization, these attacks are controlled.

Promoting Responses Incompatible with Anger and Aggression

There are two ways in which ritual specialists may help to promote responses by the bereaved that are inconsistent with anger and aggression. First of all, the specialists may provide ritual activity for the bereaved, so that time gets filled with things to do. The need for "something to do" has been discussed in some detail by Eliot (1948), Gorer (1965), and Vernon (1970: 54-55). The value of something to do in controlling anger and aggression is that it produces responses in the bereaved. As long as these responses are not anger and aggression, ritual activity by the bereaved will leave less room for responses of anger and aggression. Praying, singing, and dancing are some of the cross-culturally common bereavement behaviors that may preclude anger or attack. Additionally, as we indicated earlier in this chapter, having something to do reduces the frustration of not knowing what to do.

A second way in which ritual specialists may promote responses incompatible with anger and aggression is by defining the inchoate early feelings of grief as something other than anger. Early in bereavement, many people, especially those who have not previously been bereaved or have not previously been bereaved by a loss like the current one, experience emotions that are poorly defined for them, however intense (cf. Habenstein 1968; Vernon 1970: 170). Sarnoff and Zimbardo (1961) have argued, from a theoretical viewpoint developed by Schachter and first published by Schachter and Singer (1962), that because of uncertainty about feelings some bereaved people have a need to evaluate their reactions. This viewpoint implies that situational cues, including emotion-defining words and actions by others, are important in defining the internal feelings experienced in bereavement and in shaping overt reactions. Thus, cues could, in combination with the strong but undefined feelings, lead to a wide range of emotional expression, including laughter, sexual arousal, or other responses that for Americans are bizarre expressions of grief. Ritual specialists, both through the ritual they engineer and through their expertise, can—and presumably often do—define emotions for the bereaved as something other than anger (cf. Bowman 1959: 22-23). Ritual specialists can protect themselves, as well as others, by thus delimiting the expression of aggression (cf. Warner 1961: chap. 5). They could, of course, accomplish this delimiting by means other than the definition of emotions. For example they could argue from their positions of high authority that the expression of anger by a bereaved person is a sign of abnormality, weakness, or unholiness. Nonetheless, we think that defining emotions for the bereaved is much the more common accomplishment of ritual specialists. A content analysis of what ritual specialists—including American clergymen and funeral directors—say to the bereaved and about the bereaved within the hearing of the bereaved would, we believe, reveal a great deal of emotion-defining but rarely any indication that anger is being felt by the bereaved. Perhaps it was for this reason that the British social anthropologist Radcliffe-Brown could state with such confidence that in "primitive" communities, but apparently not in "civilized" ones such as ours, a death produces anger (Radcliffe-Brown 1964: 300).

The value of ritual specialists in controlling anger and aggression seems particularly important up to and including the initial disposal of the body. During that period, the loss is most salient, the means of coping with it least clear or least accepted by the bereaved, and the emotional feelings experienced by the bereaved least likely to have been defined (cf. Vernon 1970: 164). Hence, we believe that the more important the ritual specialists in the period up to and including initial body disposal, the less the anger and aggression expressed by the bereaved.

Institutionalized Anger and Aggression

An alternative to the reduction of anger and aggression through the use of ritual specialists is to channel anger and aggression toward institutionalized targets. We define institutionalized targets for the bereaved as persons or things that are (1) publicly recognized and tolerated targets for anger and aggression and (2) common objects for anger and aggression in bereavement. Across cultures, targets for such anger and aggression include the self, outgroup members, inanimate objects, spirits, animals, and the presumed killer of the deceased. (In some societies, every or almost every death is believed to be caused by some person.)

Institutionalized anger and aggression can create problems. For example in societies with institutionalized targets for the expression of anger and aggression, some ingroup members or allies may be potential institutionalized targets; they may be potentially definable as killers of the deceased. Furthermore, the expression of anger and aggression against one target may, as suggested by the data on anger and aggression that were reported in the previous chapter, lead to anger and aggression against others. The spread of attack from one target to another may occur simply because once one has expressed angry feelings, one may find the expression so gratifying that one is inclined to do it again. Alternatively, the spread of attack may result simply from lumping many people together in the same mental category—with thoughts such as "all these X's are alike" or "nobody is interested in my welfare." As an additional problem source, when people attack themselves or other people close to them, these attacks may be cues to further aggression and may motivate additional anger and aggression. The motivation may occur for various reasons, some of which were mentioned in the previous chapter. The pain of an attack on oneself could be angering, thereby creating additional disposition to aggress. An attack on self by a bereaved person could produce resentment directed at bereaved people who are not attacking themselves, could provide an additional source of anger if others frustrate the attack on self by trying to stop it, or could increase the intensity of undefined emotional feelings which might develop into anger and aggression. Furthermore, once an aggressive act has occurred, the diverse feelings of bereavement may more easily be defined simply as anger. Finally, when others are attacked, they may retaliate, and their retaliation may set off an exchange of attacks which seriously disrupts social cohesion.

If social relations among the living are to be preserved in societies with institutionalized anger and aggression, there must be mechanisms for delimiting noninstitutionalized violence against others. There are two customary practices which we believe could serve protective functions and which (if we are right about the need for such customs and their effectiveness) should be associated with institutionalized anger and aggression by the bereaved.

One custom is isolation or seclusion of the bereaved. Obviously, if a bereaved person is in seclusion, distant from others or separated from them by barriers, interacting with few people and perhaps minimally with them, the opportunities for attacks on others to occur or for minor frustrations in interaction to set off such attacks are minimal. Moreover, isolated people may be insulated from the ordinary environmental cues to aggression. We hypothesize that customary isolation of the bereaved serves a social control function and, consequently, is more common where there are institutionalized patterns of anger and aggression by the bereaved.

A second custom which may control institutionalized aggression is marking of the bereaved. If bereaved persons are set off from others by special dress, head shaving or hair style, scarification, uncleanliness, or some other marking of their bereaved status, others can be continually reminded to be careful in interaction with them (cf. Hocart 1931). Their carefulness may reduce the frequency of instigation to anger or aggression. Hence, we hypothesize that customary marking of the bereaved is more common where there are institutionalized patterns of anger and aggression by the bereaved. The first of the following two ethnographic passages illustrates marking, the second both marking and isolation.

> A man in deep mourning painted his entire face black; in less extreme mourning he painted a black circle covering each eye. Informants differ on the custom among women, some saying that a woman in mourning covered her face entirely with black paint, others that she painted her face with black streaks, and others stating that she used no black paint. Probably the observance was decided by the individual. The custom of cutting the hair or wearing it unbraided, and of wearing old clothing was universally observed [Densmore, "Chippewa Customs," 1929: 77]. [The Chippewa were and are found largely in Minnesota, Wisconsin, and Ontario.]

> Very close kin were expected to show their sorrow at the death of a loved one not only by crying and wailing, but also by casting off their good clothes and donning old ones — robes, for instance, consisting of pieces of old discarded lodge covers, or ordinary robes that were rough and worn — and by cutting the hair. . . .
> Close kin were accustomed to further show grief by going off to the hills and fasting, crying aloud as they wandered about alone, and sleeping out without shelter. A parent

would have done so at the loss of a son, one spouse at the death of the other, or a sister for her deceased brother [Flannery, "The Gros Ventres of Montana," 1953: 204].

It may be that both marking and isolation of the bereaved serve other functions, particularly in recruiting assistance for the bereaved and in enhancing the performance of mourning roles. It may be that the people practicing marking or isolation think that they are accomplishing something other than controlling aggression. They may, for example, believe that marking or isolation protects the bereaved from the spirit of the deceased. Nonetheless it seems valid to us to explore the possible functions of isolation and marking in controlling anger and aggression.

To review, we hypothesized first of all that: *the more important the ritual specialists up to and including initial body disposal, the less the expression of anger and aggression during mourning.* Second, we hypothesized that: *where there was institutionalized anger and aggression, there would be marking and isolation of the bereaved.*

Findings

Ritual Specialists

According to the data, anger and aggression tend to be expressed less during bereavement in societies where ritual specialists are relatively important up to and including initial body disposal. Thus, the data on ritual specialists follow the pattern suggested by the theoretical analyses earlier in this chapter. We would have liked to explore the effects of initial ritualization of funeral activities, in addition to the importance of ritual specialists, but our measure of initial ritualization failed to meet minimal technical criteria for measure adequacy. (See Appendix, section 2.1, for technical details.)

It seems appropriate at this point to discuss a salient characteristic of the societies that have a relatively high level of importance of ritual specialists in initial funeral activities. In our data, it is quite clear that ritual specialists are more likely to be present and important in large-scale societies with relatively permanent communities. There are several plausible reasons why this should be so. First of all, large-scale societies with relatively permanent communities may be in a much better position to afford specialists in anything, including specialists in ritual following a death. A larger population makes it more feasible for individuals to specialize, and large-scale, relatively permanent communities are more likely to be able to afford a food surplus, which enables the development of part-time or full-time specializations outside of the area of food production (Steward 1955: chap. 11; White 1959). Second, the risks of uncontrolled aggression may be greater in a large-scale society. We assume that in the important face-to-face relationships of one's life one (a) is frequently frustrated and (b) learns to inhibit or limit expression of aggression. One's dependence on people one sees often will further serve to curb hostility. In a small-scale society, the expression of anger and aggression during bereavement may be more controllable, because a large proportion of the contacts of a bereaved person are with people seen often. In contrast, in a large-scale society, bereaved persons will have more opportunity to be faced with potential targets of anger and aggression who are not daily intimates. The bereaved will not have had much practice at inhibiting or delimiting aggression toward such less familiar people (and these people will lack experience at tolerating aggression from the bereaved). There is, therefore, a greater risk in a large-scale society that once anger or aggression is expressed, it may be relatively uninhibited. Consequently there is more to be gained in a large-scale society from the use of any mechanism that controls anger and aggression in bereavement.

Despite these plausible arguments, it may be that there is something about large-scale societies with relatively permanent communities in addition to or alternative to ritual specialists that is responsible for the lower level of anger and aggression in bereavement in such societies. Or there may be something about small-scale societies with relatively impermanent communities other than the relative unimportance of ritual specialists that is responsible for their higher level of anger and aggression in bereavement. Perhaps the most likely "something" is that large-scale societies have cultural mechanisms for maintaining peace in a large population, with government, socialization for peace with ingroup members, religious doctrine (Swanson 1960: chap. 9), and other factors all working to control overt anger and aggression. It may be these other factors in large-scale societies, rather than ritual specialists, that delimit anger and aggression in bereavement. However, we have no evidence on this point, and it may well be that ritual specialists are important in producing the apparent peace-keeping effects, if there are any, of government, socialization for ingroup peace, and religious doctrine.

Isolation

Isolation of widows is strongly related to institutionalized attacks, either verbally or physically, by new widows of some institutionalized target (including self). Isolation of widowers is strongly related to institutionalized attacks by widowers of some target. However, isolation of adult offspring who are mourning for their own parents is not statistically associated with measures of institutionalized anger and aggression, nor is isolation of parents who are mourning for subadult offspring associated with parental attacks on some institutionalized target. (See Appendix, section 2.1, for technical details.)

Isolation of adult offspring occurs in only three of thirty-four societies for which isolation of adult offspring could be rated, and isolation of parents who are mourning for subadult offspring occurs in only three of thirty-six cases for which that variable could be rated. By contrast, widows are isolated in nineteen of forty cases, and widowers are isolated in twelve of thirty-six cases. Perhaps aggressive emotional reactions are more intense for bereaved spouses than for bereaved parents and adult offspring. It is possible, for example, that frustration and consequent disposition to anger and aggression are less when a person dies who, like a small child or an elderly person, is less productive economically or whose death has broken fewer or weaker ties. Or perhaps isolation is too burdensome for societies with high death rates for infants and children or with elderly persons who leave many surviving offspring.

Marking

Marking of widows is associated statistically with two measures of institutionalized anger and aggression, and marking of parents of a deceased subadult offspring is associated statistically with institutionalized attack on something by parents of deceased subadult offspring. For the other categories of mourner, marking is not related to institutionalized anger and aggression. (Technical details of these analyses can be found in the Appendix, section 2.1.)

Isolation vs. Marking

There is a possibility that isolation and marking are to some extent alternatives to each other in delimiting institutionalized anger and aggression. First of all, we note that isolation of widowers is strongly associated with institutionalized anger and aggression by widowers, but that marking is not. In contrast, marking of bereaved parents is associated with institutionalized anger and aggression, but isolation is not. Secondly, marking is present for bereaved parents in twelve of twenty-one cases, while isolation is present in only three of thirty-six cases. Aggression by a man who has lost his wife may not be adequately controlled by marking, while isolation may be dysfunctional and unnecessary for bereaved parents in the many societies in which infant and child mortality rates are high.

Marking and isolation do seem to occur where we have hypothesized that they would be useful for bereaved spouses and for parents of subadult offspring. We analyzed data for adult offspring of the deceased, but found no association of marking or isolation with institutionalized anger and aggression. This may mean that the threat of spread of anger and aggression when an elderly parent dies is relatively low. The ties between adult offspring and their parents may often have become comparatively tenuous, due either to the normal extrusion from a dependent relationship as one matures or to the possibility that the deaths of elderly parents might often be anteceded by a prolonged decline in health, which might produce substantial adjustment to loss in the period before the death.

Deviant Case Analysis

We have assumed that societies either deal with their important problems or get into trouble. We have further assumed that anger and aggression during bereavement were important problems and that societies would either have customs that deal with anger and aggression in bereavement or would suffer consequences, such as high murder rates and disruption of family relations and alliances.

If our basic theoretical notions are correct, societies with institutionalized anger and aggression but lacking isolation and marking must either have a functional alternative to isolation and marking or must suffer from a high level of disruption. If our basic theoretical notions are correct, there should be no society in which ritual specialists are important and patterns of institutionalized anger and aggression are present—unless there are functional alternatives to ritual specialists. To probe the limits of our theoretical analysis, we searched our data for deviant cases.

There is one society in our data with important ritual specialists and with some form of institutionalized anger and aggression, the Egyptian Fellahin (peasants). For them, institutionalized anger and aggression seem to be present for widows and adult female siblings of the deceased. According to Blackman (1927: 114, 123), women dancing in grief customarily slap their own faces. At times, some women draw blood. By our theorizing, this self-directed aggression is a puzzle. The ritual specialists should be associated with conditions that minimize the expression of anger and aggression. Blackman gives no indication of any factor that could promote this self-aggression despite the activity of ritual specialists. Nor does she write of escalating anger and aggression by the women who have been slapping their own faces. It would be useful to have more data. One possibility is that the face slapping is not understood by the people who practice it to be an expression of anger; i.e. the face slapping may be defined as something sorrowful or rhythmical but not angry. Nonetheless, it seems that ritual specialists may not be sufficient to eliminate the expression of anger and aggression.

There is only one society in our sample that has institution-

alized anger and aggression for a category of bereaved person
but lacks both marking and isolation for that category of
person—the Cubeo, a small-scale, Tucano-speaking people
of the Northwest Amazon basin. Examination of the ethnographic materials describing the Cubeo, materials from the
work of Irving Goldman (1948, 1963), indicates that the Cubeo
are plagued with the problems that our theoretical analysis
argues they should have in the absence of adequate control
of institutionalized anger and aggression. There seems to be
a substantial amount of disruptive aggression, constituting
a serious challenge to the integrity of Cubeo communities.

Among the Cubeo, death by illness is attributed to sorcery.
The pattern of institutionalized anger and aggression includes
(1) the expression of anger at the sorcerer and (2) a ritual in-
quest, accompanied by angry funeral orations. If a specfic
sorcerer is identified and apprehended in the period immediately following the death, he will probably be killed. The
risk in this pattern can be read in Goldman's words:

> When the fear of sorcery begins to grow, accusations may
> strike within the sib and split it down the middle [Goldman,
> 1963: 218].

> The fear of sorcery constitutes an ever-present threat to the
> stability of social relations, even within the individual family.
> All illness and non-violent death is attributed to sorcery, and
> such an occurrence invariably provokes bitter recriminations
> and open battles. Among the *Cubeo*, sibs have often been re-
> duced to a mere handful of people following the accusation
> that they practice sorcery. Fear of sorcery not infrequently
> interferes with ceremonies and sometimes restricts attendance
> at drinking parties, which are ordinarily popular, to members
> of the immediate household [Goldman, 1948: 797].

Cubeo sorcery accusations and fears surrounding a death can
lead to mounting aggression and disruption of social relations.
If the most bereaved persons were isolated, some of the disruptive aggression might be avoided. Although it is difficult
to see how marking could make much difference in a society
with such a high level of tension, it is possible that if the
most bereaved persons were isolated, some of the disruptive
aggression might be avoided. To some extent, disruptive
aggression seems to be limited by the behavior of nonbereaved

persons, who avoid drinking parties attended by bereaved persons. But apparently that is not enough, and the cost of anger and aggression in bereavement seems substantial for the Cubeo.

Controlling the Anger and Aggression of Bereavement in the United States

Our data suggest important things about bereavement in the United States. At deaths, ritual specialists—particularly physicians, clergymen, nurses, and funeral directors—dominate customs up to and including the initial body disposal. As is true of other societies in which ritual specialists dominate, anger and aggression seem not to be expressed with great frequency in the United States. Although feelings of anger are probably present commonly, it is conceivable that they would be much more frequently expressed and much more intense if ritual specialists were absent.

For people thinking of moving away from customary American funeral services toward individualistic services (cf. Mitford 1963), our data and theory suggest that there is a risk. The risk is that, in the absence of substantial involvement of ritual specialists, anger and aggression might be much more of a problem than they usually are in the United States. The crucial variable, however, seems not to be whether one moves to unconventional services but whether bereaved persons are left on their own or experience considerable intervention by ritual specialists, conventional or unconventional.

If expression of anger were encouraged early in bereavement in the United States, limiting the scope and intensity of expression of emotion might be a problem. Mere aggression catharsis, without additional controls, seems to be rare cross-culturally and may lead to problems of snowballing hostility and violence where it does occur. Anger catharsis seems increasingly to be promoted in the United States (see, for example, the encouragement of catharsis in an undated flyer distributed by the American Funeral Directors Association, "The Condolence or Sympathy Visit"). The most typical form of catharsis that is encouraged is verbal expression of angry feelings—at self, the deceased, physicians, funeral directors, and so on. If such catharsis is to be promoted, it might be well to plan on controlling it, either through isolation (i.e. restriction of frequency and type of social contacts between bereaved and others) or through marking. The encouragement of catharsis without the addition of controls seems to risk a situation more like that of the Cubeo than is presently the case in the United States (see further discussion of catharsis in Chapter 7).

Neither isolation nor marking may be difficult to institutionalize in the United States. According to Lindemann (1944), bereaved Americans tend to avoid others in order to avoid the discomfort that follows references to the deceased and in order to avoid being irritable or distant in social relations. Isolation of the bereaved may also occur in America in the sense that the formality of condolence calls, condolence cards, and funeral visitation may produce a pattern of restricted interaction with newly bereaved persons. Lopata (1973: 188-89) reports that some American widows experience reduced contact with their acquaintances following the onset of widowhood. This may be evidence of isolation. However, some widows may feel themselves becoming more isolated simply because they received an abnormally large amount of attention and support at the onset of bereavement. Then, after their acquaintances have worked off their feelings of obligation, the widows are returned to a more normal amount of contact, which they may experience as a decrease.

Isolation of the bereaved in the United States could conceivably be institutionalized in the sense of becoming publicly recognized and supported. Institutionalization might also help to reduce some problems of bereavement. People who isolate themselves and are isolated or distanced for reasons that all understand and accept need feel less anxiety and anger over the isolation and may, at some future date when the isolation is ended (see Chapter 5 for a discussion of formally ending mourning), more easily resume relations with those from whom they have been separated. Institutionalizing isolation for a clearly defined period might also reduce the ambivalence that bereaved persons and their acquaintances feel over the involvement of the bereaved in social activities.

Marking at one time was institutionalized in various ways for Americans of European origin, particularly through the wearing of black. Americans in mourning may still often dress more soberly. Among British widows studied by Hobson (1964), and by Marris (1958), the majority reported dressing more soberly for at least three months after the husband's death. Comparable data on dressing more soberly have been reported for American widows by Glick, Weiss, and Parkes (1974: 120-22). To move toward the institutionalization of isolation or marking may be comparatively easy. People can be reminded that these activities are or were common and traditional and can also be educated in the possible value of the activities. Of course, such a campaign would need the support of religious and secular authorities and would require some mechanism, such as a final funeral ceremony (Chapter 5), for ending the period of marking or isolation.

Chapter Summary

In this chapter we have argued that dispositions toward anger and aggression are universal components of bereavement. To control these dispositions, societies may employ ritual specialists, whose ritual guidance of the bereaved helps to curtail the expression of anger and aggression in a number of ways. Alternatively, societies may allow institutionalized expression of anger and aggression, coupled with control on the spread of anger and aggression through the use of marking or isolation of the bereaved. The data provide support for this analysis. We have discussed the implications of the theory and data for American practices, including the activities of ritual specialists such as funeral directors and the increasingly common encouragement of hostility catharsis in bereavement.

Part 2. Ties to the Deceased:

Symptoms and Tie-Breaking

In the three chapters of this section of the book, we discuss the residues of relationship left behind by a person who dies. We point to various manifestations of those residues and discuss some cultural devices for reducing and eventually minimizing the effects of the residues. Here we would like to outline the ways in which the chapters of this section meet the overall aims of the book.

The first of our aims has been to identify what is fundamentally human. In the following three chapters, we point to two things that seem to be fundamentally human in bereaved persons—to have ghost beliefs or cognitions and to respond to familiar stimuli in ways that would only be appropriate if the deceased were still alive.

The second aim of this book has been to identify cultural responses to needs created by a death. In these chapters, we consider two cultural devices that reduce and eventually minimize ties to the deceased: (1) separation from or alteration of familiar cues to respond to the deceased and (2) funeral ceremonies that help to terminate the ties to the deceased. A subsidiary aim has been to identify cultural factors that affect what cultural responses are made to needs created by a death. We meet this subsidiary aim by considering the role of permanence of housing in whether abandoning the house of the deceased is a customary means of breaking ties with the deceased.

The third goal of the book, to try to understand cross-culturally common death customs, is also met in these chapters. The customs dealt with include destruction and disposal of personal property of the deceased, practicing a taboo on the name of the deceased, abandonment of a dwelling or a room of a dwelling previously inhabited by the deceased, and final funeral ceremonies occurring substantially after the initial ceremonies.

The fourth goal of the book, to put American customs and experiences in perspective, is achieved in three major ways by this section of the book. We raise the question of whether American denial of the possibility of ghost cognitions in normal people might be creating problems for many bereaved persons. We discuss the paucity of customs in the United States to help bereaved persons break ties with the deceased. And we point to the possible cost of there being no customary time-limiting of mourning in the United States.

Chapter 3

Ghosts

All the men of our family dug the grave, and then carried him out and put him there. They put in his blanket and pillow, because we did not sleep on mats any more. And his leather pouch, they put in, and the sticks he had for games and his bow and arrows and his good quiver of wild cat skin. Then his brother spoke: "We put you here. Stay and don't come back to frighten us." My mother said: "Make yourself at home. Be happy. Don't come back to break up my good dreams." She was crying. Then we called him again. "Haya, my father!" "Haya, my elder brother!" "Haya, my husband." [Underhill, "The Autobiography of a Papago Woman," 1936: 50].

This chapter deals with ghost beliefs. We define ghost beliefs as being present if people in a culture typically believe either that ghosts, spirits, apparitions, or other manifestations of specific deceased persons are themselves capable of being perceived or that the results of actions by such entities are capable of being perceived.

Four raters were asked whether or not ghost beliefs, as we defined them, were present in the societies studied. Of the sixty-six societies for which information was available to the raters and for which we had substantial rater agreement on presence or absence of ghost beliefs, ghost beliefs were rated present in sixty-five. Only the Masai were rated as lacking ghost beliefs, and the Masai society was next-to-last among our seventy-eight societies in the amount of ethnographic material about grief and mourning we had available to us, as indicated by the proportion of the first 118 variables we measured on which it could be rated. Thus, ghost beliefs seem to us to be nearly universal (if not universal) cross-culturally.

That ghost beliefs are present in a society is not indicative of the percentage of dead persons who are believed to leave behind a ghost or of the percentage of people who ever believe that they have perceived a ghost or the actions of a ghost. Ghosts may actually be perceived as appearing very rarely. We know of no systematic studies of the cognitive and motivational processes underlying ghost cognitions and beliefs in cultures where ghost cognitions and beliefs are acceptable in normal people. It is, therefore, impossible to offer an empirically tested explanation of cross-cultural variations in the incidence of ghost cognitions and beliefs. However, people in some cultures believe that they can reduce the frequency of their own ghost cognitions through protective practices that are calculated to keep ghosts away. The following ethnographic quotations illustrate such protective practices.

> The Walbiri generally count uncircumcised boys and unmarried girls as children; and, when a child dies, only those country-men present at the time are specifically involved in the activities that follow. Actual or close mother's mothers or, less often, elder sisters (that is, women of the matriline) bury the corpse quickly and without formality in a shallow, unmarked grave in the bush near the parents' dwelling. The women are not ritually cleansed afterwards. The parents, in order to avoid the attentions of the ghost (which is the deceased's matrispirit in mobile form), vacate their shelter at once and build another about a quarter or half a mile away. Should the dead child have been very young, they simply leave the old shelter to decay. But if the child was more than three or four years old and had a personal name, its ghost is thought to be rather more dangerous. The parents, therefore, burn their old dwelling; and all their neighbours (their countrymen) also shift camp for a few hundred yards [Meggitt, *Desert People*, 1965: 318]. [The Walbiri are an Australian aboriginal group.]

> After a death, the camp is speedily moved, often to a distance of several miles, this being for fear of the dead person's spirit, which is called *kemoid*. It is liable to enter the huts and kill people because it regards them as relatives. It is white and cannot speak, but can be seen. The dead eat only the shadows of things. They sleep in the daytime and wander at night in

search of food [Evans, *The Negritos of Malaya*, 1937: 263].
[The group described is known as the Semang.]

The fact that ghost beliefs are present in all but one of the
societies that raters could agree upon is startling. In the
United States, ghosts are a topic for jokes, fanciful films,
and fiction. To admit to the belief that one has perceived
a ghost or the action of a ghost is to invite being labeled as
ignorant, superstitious, irrational, or hallucinating. It is
sobering to find American culture so much in the minority
on this issue (cf. Kalish and Reynolds 1973). What the cross-
cultural literature seems to indicate is that belief in ghosts
is natural; it is consistent with human nature. It seems to us,
moreover, that the widespread presence of ghost beliefs is
explicable in terms of contemporary behavioral science. First
of all, many environmental cues will have been associated in
the mind of a surviving person with the presence of a deceased
person who was known well. A man in the United States, for
example, may have learned that the sound of a car door slam-
ming in front of his house at 5:30 on a weekday afternoon
usually signals the entry of his wife into the house. Her presence will be cued at other times by innumerable other
stimuli—by a squeak of the floor in a nearby room, the sound
of water running in the plumbing, the sounds and sights
of a suppertime newscast, the sounds from outside the house
in the early morning, the smell of cookies baking, and so on.
If such associations have been learned, it is plausible that
those stimuli might set off a sense of her presence even after
she died. For a moment the man imagines his wife to be present or senses that somehow she is nearby. Thus, a simple view
of associative learning would lead us to expect people often
to have a sense of the presence of a ghost after the death of a
familiar person.

We would also expect ghost perceptions to develop out of
both day and night dreams (cf. Avebury 1902: 226-27; Hertz
1960: 150, n. 319; Hobson 1964; Kastenbaum and Aisenberg
1972: 180; Mitchell 1967: 103-04). People might be expected
to dream frequently about people close to them who have
died (Clayton 1975). The unconscious does not seem likely
to eliminate a significant person from one's dream world

simply because that person is no longer present. As Freud wrote:

> When a man has lost someone dear to him, for a considerable period afterwards he produces a special type of dream, in which the most remarkable compromises are effected between his knowledge that that person is dead and his desire to call him back to life. Sometimes the deceased is dreamt of as being dead, and yet still alive because he does not know that he is dead, as if he would only really die if he did know it; at other times he is half dead and half alive, and each of these conditions has its distinguishing marks. We must not call these dreams merely nonsensical . . . [1949: 196-97].

We have not been able to find in the work of Freud the idea that people do not always keep separate their memories of dreams and their memories of realities, but to the extent that memories of dreams merge with memories of reality and to the extent that people blur the boundary between dream occurrences and reality occurrences when coming out of a dream, we would expect fantasy life to produce ghost cognitions. In some cultures, the appearance of a deceased person in a dream is taken as evidence of actual contact by the dreamer with the spirit of the deceased person. Consider the following passage.

> In standardized dreams, a prominent part is played by visions of departed spirits. They appear to people in sleep under appropriate circumstances and at certain seasons. This is in fact one of the chief ways in which they manifest their existence to the living. But not all dreams about the departed are regarded as true. The appearance may be either a *sasopa* (lie, illusion) or a real *baloma* (spirit). Real spirits always come with a purpose and under conditions in which they can properly be expected. Thus if a recently dead person appears in sleep to a surviving relative, giving him some important message or announcing his death at a distance—such a dream is true [Malinowski, *The Sexual Life of Savages*, 1969: 387-88]. [This passage deals with the people of the Trobriand Islands, an archipelago off the northeast coast of New Guinea.]

Self-perception theory (Bem 1972) provides another basis for expecting some people to have ghost beliefs. The theory says that people make guesses about perceptions, emotions, and other internal states by drawing inferences from what they find themselves doing. For example a person who finds himself kissing another would tend to infer that he is feeling affection, liking, or sexual desire. A person finding himself working very hard toward some end will tend to infer that he values that end. Now consider a person who finds himself thinking about a deceased relative and speaking aloud as though the relative were still alive. Or consider a man lying in the bed he shared with his now-deceased spouse, thinking about her, and finding himself sexually aroused. Self-perception theory would lead us to expect some people in such situations to tend to infer that they have perceived some kind of manifestation of the deceased. In searching for an explanation of the talking aloud or the sexual arousal, some people might come to believe that they were responding to a manifestation of the deceased.

Then, too, an interaction with a ghost could conceivably serve various ego needs. For example one could transact unfinished emotional, relational, or decision-making business with the deceased (Blauner 1966; Matchett 1972). If needs to finish such business can influence people to develop ghost perceptions, or cognitions, then that constitutes another reason to expect some people to believe that they have been in contact with a ghost.

Consistent with all these explanations of the commonality of ghost beliefs are the cross-cultural data we have on the extent to which the ghosts that people perceive are of people they knew best. For the thirty-five societies that our raters could rate with agreement, thirty-three, or 94 percent. were societies in which the ghosts that people perceive are of people they knew best. Ghost cognitions seem to arise preponderantly out of the residues of close social relationships, which is consistent with our explanations of the commonality of ghost cognitions or beliefs. It is the dead people that one knew well whose presence would be most likely to be cued by one's surroundings, who would be most likely to appear in dreams, who would be most likely to be the focus of responses that need an explanation, and with whom one would be most likely to have unfinished business. The following passage dealing with a Fijian community and the passage later on in this chapter that deals with the Tikopia may give the reader a more vivid sense of the degree to which the ghosts in people's lives are the ghosts of familiar people.

> The soul of one who has died may wreak vengeance upon his kinsmen if they fail to observe funeral ceremonies with propriety. The soul of a chief is more dangerous than that of a commoner; an adult's is more dangerous than a child's. For many weeks after a death people avoid solitude after dark. Some six-year-olds once scampered into a house in which the men were drinking kava informally; Samu said: "Aren't you afraid to be running about after dark? There are dead souls about. Sakiusa is lurking in the path." After Vilomena's death women hastened home from fishing expeditions to reach the village before dark. When anyone went to the river at night, he carried a torch or a lantern and usually persuaded a guard of companions to accompany him. If the wind dislodged a bucket from its hanging and sent it clattering to the ground, or if a sudden gust smote the mat hangings of a doorway which had been closed against the rain, someone would surely say: "Vilomena is about." And people would shiver as their own souls, uncomfortable in the presence of a dead soul, lifted the hair at the backs of their necks. Once at dusk on the Lekutu path far from the village Peni felt his soul climb high upon his neck as signal that a dead soul was near by; Peni shuddered in disgust and, as he hurried his steps, shouted insults over his shoulder to frighten the dead soul. He knew intuitively that it was the soul of Sakiusa, his beloved sister's child, who came seeking him. But, as time passes, souls of the dead become ridiculous. Small accidents were attributed laughingly to Vilomena and Sakiusa. The children made a game, and, pretending that Vilomena was chasing them, they raced about the village green in delicious terror.
> A child is in special danger when a parent dies lest this parent return in loneliness to carry off the child's soul. When Bici's mother died, Bici took his present name as nickname so that his dead mother would not recognize him when she came seeking. Yet Vilomena's mentally retarded eight-year-old daughter Unaisi knew no fear. Because she was sired in the path by a wandering Solomon Islander, people were not surprised that she failed to understand what other children knew. It amused them when in her piping voice she babbled about her mother as though she had not died, but finally they made her hush because they feared the anger of Vilomena's soul [Quain, *Fijian Village*, 1948: 373].

In light of the cross-cultural data indicating universality or

near-universality of ghost beliefs, and in light of the plausible behavioral science arguments for the presence of ghost
beliefs or cognitions, we must wonder what denial by Americans and Europeans of the reality of ghost beliefs or cognitions
might do to bereaved people. Perhaps these pressures against
ghost beliefs make it unlikely that people will have ghost
beliefs or cognitions, but we think it likely that many bereaved
Americans and Europeans have ghost cognitions or experience what they suspect are manifestations of somebody deceased. In support of this, there are data from a survey of an
unsystematically drawn sample of professionals who work
with the bereaved (Heimlich and Kutscher 1970). Three-
quarters of the professionals anticipated that the bereaved
would experience illusions of the deceased at least some of
the time. In a related study of bereaved persons, Kutscher
(1970) stated that half of the bereaved persons investigated
reported that illusions of the deceased occur at least at some
time. In both studies, 90 percent of the respondents anticipated that dreams of the deceased would occur at some time.
In a study of twenty-two London widows (Parkes 1970, 1972),
ten thought they heard or saw their husband during the
first month after his death, and sixteen of the twenty-two
widows had a sense of the presence of their husbands near
them. Comparable data on sense-of-presence have been reported by Clayton, Desmarais, and Winokur (1968), Glick,
Weiss, and Parkes (1974), Hobson (1964), Marris (1958, 1974),
Rees (1971), and Wretmark (1959). Matchett (1972) concluded
from a study of Hopi Indian widows that ghost cognitions are
common in human experience, and Krupp and Kligfeld (1962)
have also observed that feeling the presence of the deceased is
common. Thus, despite the overt American and European
rejection of ghost cognitions and beliefs, there are clinical
data from America and Europe that are consistent with the
cross-cultural data. Ghost cognitions and beliefs are very
human.

It seems likely, then, that the American and European attitude toward ghost beliefs and cognitions creates problems
for bereaved persons. To admit to having a conversation with
a deceased person or to having seen a supposedly buried person
sitting in one's living room is very risky in American society.

Consequently, many bereaved persons may be unable to talk with others about this area of experience and potential anxiety (cf. Rees 1971). Furthermore, many may be led to doubt their own sanity by experiences of ghost cognitions, which would of course add to the burden of their loss. Doubt of personal sanity has, in fact, been observed commonly in bereaved persons (Lindemann 1944), though not to our knowledge ever clearly attributed in whole or in part to ghost cognitions. Perhaps problems with ghost cognitions contribute to the mental and physical problems so frequently observed in bereaved persons (Averill 1968; Gorer 1965). If professionals who work with bereaved persons were alerted to the likelihood of ghost cognitions, they might be in a position to reduce distress in many bereaved persons and, once they had shown that they were accepting of such "deviant" mental processes, to learn much more from bereaved persons about thought processes during bereavement. We hope that greater acceptance by professionals and lay persons of ghost cognitions will result from the cross-cultural information presented in this book.

Ghost Fear

We asked our raters to note whether fear of ghosts was present. These ratings have already been discussed to some extent in Chapter 1. The instructions to the raters stated that ghost fear was to be rated as present "if adults are generally afraid of the spirit of the typical dead adult at some time." Thus, the ratings were focused on ghosts of typical dead adults, not at an unusual ghost that might be frightening, such as the ghost of a person who had been thought to be a witch. Fear was counted as present if people were fearful in anticipation of a ghost appearing, even if ghosts rarely or never appeared. Fear was also counted as present where people were fearful of ghosts harming them if ceremonies were done improperly. Fear was defined as "painful agitation in the presence or anticipation of danger."

The ratings of fear of ghosts were made by four raters. As was indicated in Chapter 1, the raters were able to generate ratings of presence-absence of fear of ghosts for forty-four societies, and ghost fear was judged to be present in thirty-seven of these. We assume that the societies that could not be rated on ghost fear are merely poorly described and not, for example, cases in which people generally fear ghosts and wish to hide that fear from ethnographers, from ghosts, or from each other. And we assume that the cases that could not be rated are not cases in which ethnographers reported nothing about fear because (1) they believed that people generally do not fear ghosts (2) they observed no ghost fear in the societies they were studying, and (3) the absence of ghost fear seemed to them to be so unremarkable that they did not report it.

It seems from our data that Bendann (1930: 57) and Frazer (1933-36), who both asserted that ghost fear is *universal* in human societies, were wrong. Nonetheless, ghost fear seems to occur in the preponderance of societies (in eighty-four percent of our forty-four ratable societies), and its commonality seems to us to be a fact worth explaining.

Explanations of Ghost Fear Applicable in all Societies

Four plausible explanations of ghost fear have direct implications for any bereaved person who experiences ghost cognitions. One of these explanations is that ghost fear is a normal reaction to the discrepancy between the fact of death and the apparent presence as if alive in some form of the person supposedly dead. Such an explanation might be especially applicable to societies such as ours, wherein the dead are defined as incapable of action in the world of the living. In societies with belief systems that allow more tolerance of people who experience ghost cognitions, reactions to ghost cognitions might more often be surprise, pleasure, or something else different from fear. Consider, for example, the following passage dealing with the Tikopia, a Polynesian people.

> [One ghost] was that of a young man, unmarried and a pagan, who fell from a high cliff while climbing to net birds nesting on the rock face. His spirit appeared on various occasions, causing talk and some fright. But the attitude of Tikopia to such apparitions is often very matter-of-fact. The

lad was regarded as having lost his life through foolhardy
tempting of his skill, and judgement on this comes out in the
spirit encounters. A friend of mine told me how the lad appeared in spirit form to one of his kinsfolk who was awake in
his house at night. He called out "Brother" and the living
man recognized the voice of the dead. He replied in a curse,
"Here you are coming and calling out to me—I excrete in
your gullet." Then the ghost went away. . . . Another of his
kinsfolk had a similar experience when the ghost opened the
door of his house. He called out something that, freely translated, was, "You fool, what have you come peering in here
for? It was your own stupid fault that you went and fell off
the cliff." Rebuffed again, the ghost then went on to the cook-
house of his father's dwelling, and finding his father absent
he apparently began to wail and was heard crying by people.
He is said to have pulled aside the doors of several houses
[Firth, *Tikopia Ritual and Belief*, 1967: 347].

The second explanation of the commonality of ghost fear that is
applicable to all societies rests on the assumption that a bereaved
person perceives action by a ghost and accepts it as real or
probably real. Once one accepts that the dead can act in the
world of the living, one must worry about action the dead
might take against the living. One could be fearful because
one's past relationship with the dead person was not totally satisfying to the dead person, and that might lead the dead person
to take revenge (cf. Goody 1962: 90). Or one could be fearful
simply because the dead person may have some desires that
must be met in order for the survivor to avoid retribution from
the dead person.

A third explanation of ghost fear is rather commonly offered
to ethnographers by informants and might be relevant to the
fears of some bereaved persons in the United States. It is that
the past affinity between the now dead and the still living may
lead the dead to want to bring the living to join them (cf. Goody
1962: 89-90). Such joining would require death or something
similar to it. The fear of ghosts would then arise out of not
wanting to join the dead (and a bereaved person may be particularly aware of his or her own vulnerability to death) or out
of finding oneself wanting to join the dead and fearing the implications of that. See, for example, the quotes earlier in this
chapter from materials dealing with the Walbiri and the Semang
and the following quote from the Azande.

. . . the Azande say:

Guni nabi gumeni	He who sees a relation
rogo mosumo,	in a dream,
ni tuna ka gunde agunde,	is seized by a great fear,
ki ya: "Gumeru niye	and thinks: "His relation has come
ka dia ru fuo ni."	to take him with him."
Tipa ka bata be gu pai re,	To save himself from this fate,
ni nikadua tuka fu gumeni	he will build the altar to his
	relative

[Gero, *Death among the Azande of the Sudan,* 1968: 102].

A fourth explanation rests on the fact that fear of ghosts seems to promote the breaking of ties with the deceased. Tie-breaking is discussed in detail in the next chapter, where it is argued that fearing the ghost of the deceased alters the meaning of reminders of the deceased. Alteration of the meaning of reminders of the deceased would promote the resumption of a normal life without the person who has died. Consider, for example, the case of a woman whose husband has died. His tools, the structure in which he lived, the mat on which he slept, and his other possessions would be reminders of him. Without fear of his ghost, the old responses that these stimuli used to evoke in her might continue to be evoked for a comparatively long time. To the extent that the old responses are now inappropriate, she would behave inappropriately, experience feelings of loss, disruption, incompetence, and grief, and be inhibited from doing new things, such as performing a household task that her husband used to do for her or exploring the possibility of developing a martial relationship with somebody else. However, if the reminders of the deceased evoke feelings of fear, because they remind her of a fearful ghost or because they have the potentiality of bringing near her a fearful ghost, she will be motivated to cut the psychological associations between the possessions and the deceased or to separate herself from the reminders of him. Thus, one possibility for explaining the high incidence of ghost fear is that it is useful in motivating people to break ties with the deceased and to resume a normal adult life. Such useful practices can become institutionalized in societies through any of a wide range of conceivable mechanisms. Perhaps if Americans who are bereaved become free to admit ghost beliefs and ghost fears, we may find that those who have strong ghost fears will work hard to break ties with the deceased and will be likely to do things as a result of the fear, such as dispose of personal possessions of the deceased, that will help them to break those ties.

Explanations for Societies with Institutionalized Ghost Fear

The remaining three explanations seem much more applicable to societies with institutionalized ghost fear. One of these explanations for ghost fear is that it promotes the performance of death ceremonies which are valuable for the bereaved individuals and for the society at large but difficult or inconvenient for people to perform. The belief that a ghost will punish people if ceremonies are improper or omitted is common (cf. van Gennep 1960: 160 and our discussion in Chapter 5). Such a belief might lead, for example, to the holding of an expensive ceremony which promotes societal cohesion and adjustment of bereaved persons.

A second explanation of ghost fear in societies with institutionalized ghost fear arises from Perry's (1972) suggestion for the Western Apache that ghost fear is useful in scattering families following a death. Such dispersion of families, he argues, maintains an adaptive degree of kin group flexibility by making it difficult to form rigid, unilineal kin groups. Instead of nuclear families clustering together and, over the years, forming a rigidly organized group that may be locked into a suboptimal social and ecological niche, the families disperse after a death and are as a consequence free to be opportunistic about where and with whom they live. He may be right for the Western Apache, but ghost fear occurs in many societies with a good deal of kin group rigidity and strong unilineal kinship organization. The Western Apache were not tied down by their mode of subsistence or their ecology to specific pieces of land; hence, for them, dispersion of families might create relatively little hardship. But many of the societies in our sample that have substantial ghost fear are agricultural, tied to specific pieces of land, and possessing of permanent or semipermanent housing. In such societies, dispersion would be difficult, while the formation of relatively enduring kin groups would be easy and useful. The Ifugao are one example, with impressive, permanent rice terraces and an apparent depth of genealogical memory of at least ten generations (Barton 1969: 2-3). Although they have bilateral kin groups, their groups have both continuity and a corporate character. In our sample, other strong counterexamples to the Western Apache are the Thonga and the Lolo, both of which have substantial fear of ghosts and stability of social structural ties. Although we did not study systematically the relationship between fear and stability of social structure, it appears that ghost fear does not necessarily work in the service of dispersion of kin groups and of flexibility of interfamily relations. In fact, fear of ghosts can promote stability by providing the occasion of very elaborate funeral ceremonies, ostensibly to protect people and things from a ghost and to purify people and things contaminated by the death. Such ceremonies could serve to tie people together, to renew bonds, to legitimate ongoing relations, and otherwise to promote the stability of kin groups.

A final explanation of ghost fear in societies with institutionalized ghost fear is that ghost fear may recruit assistance for bereaved persons. Their danger and vulnerability may lead to behavior on the part of others in the society to protect them, thereby meeting the dependence needs that are so substantial in bereaved persons.

Eventual Distance of the Spirits

We were interested in determining where, in the beliefs of the people in the societies we studied, ghosts eventually go. It is possible for people to believe that ghosts are present on a permanent basis in the world of the living, that they go far away and then return to stay, that they vacillate in being near at times and far at others, or that they move farther away over time. Various psychological arguments led us to believe that the last alternative would predominate.

If ghost beliefs are a consequence, in part, of association of certain stimuli with memories of the deceased, we would expect that reduction of these associations through tie-breaking activities would make ghosts seem farther away as time passes. Tie-breaking activities, which are discussed in detail in the next chapter, alter the meaning of reminders of the deceased or separate the survivors from the reminders. To the extent that such activities work effectively, over the long run the ghost of the deceased should seem present less often or not at all. Normal extinction or counter-conditioning of associations involving other reminders would also reduce the extent to which survivors think of the deceased. For example the car door slam at 5:30 and the squeak in the floor in the next room would no longer be reminders of the deceased spouse. The deceased never appears after the car door slams or the squeak occurs; other events come to be more strongly associated with the noises. Consequently, over time there would develop the feeling that the ghost is not present. These psychological processes are often supplemented by rites of passage for the deceased (van Gennep 1960: chap. VIII). In the minds of those attending, such rites move the deceased from the world of the living to the world of spirits and, frequently, move the deceased to a geographically distant place. Such symbolic geographic movement seems to us to strengthen other tie-breaking activities or to be a symptom that other tie-breaking activities are working properly.

We measured eventual distance of ghosts and found the eventual distance, as expected, to be relatively far from the living in the majority of measurable societies. In twelve of the fourteen societies for which at least three of our four raters could make a rating and agreed, spirits eventually were farther from the living than they were immediately after death. Hertz (1960: 34) reports a similar finding. Our two deviant cases in eventual distance of the spirits are the Carib and the Chinese of Kaihsienkung village, Yunnan Province. An analysis of these deviant cases suggests that it might be useful to expand our concept of movement of the spirits beyond mere imagined geographical movement of the spirits.

Carib ghosts do not move away from the dwelling in which they resided while alive, but all the survivors leave the area by the time several weeks have passed. Thus, over time, a bereaved person becomes more distant from the ghost of a deceased spouse or kinsman, but this is through movement of the bereaved person, not through movement of the ghost.

There is very little information on spirits in the sources on China that were used by our raters. However, a detailed study by Emily Ahern (1973) of Chinese death customs and beliefs, with special attention to a Hokkien-speaking group in northern Taiwan, suggests that psychological distance between the living and the dead becomes greater over time, even though physical distance does not. In Chapter 13 of her book, Ahern describes spirtualist-assisted communication with the deceased, during which the spirits distance the survivor attempting the communication by means of unresponsiveness and of abrupt cutting off of interaction. Of course, the communication problems develop out of the imagination of the survivor. Ahern asserts that by experiencing this distancing and describing it to others, the survivor "is outwardly and publicly admitting what he has known inwardly since the death; the close, emotion-laden ties of dependence and support between kin can never be renewed [Ahern 1973: 244]." Thus, even though ancestor worship continues, and even though, from time to time, many ancestors inhabit the area in which the survivors live, psychological distance is increased. Possibly such distancing occurred in Kaihsienkung as well, though there is not any relevant data in the materials we used.

Although the Chinese case we used is not well enough described to enable any confident explanation of its deviance, the Carib and the Chinese cases both push us to expand our notion of movement of the spirits to include distancing through movement of the survivors and through psychological separation as represented in reduction in communication.

Chapter Summary

In this chapter we argue that ghost beliefs and cognitions arise from the normal psychological residues that remain after a close social relationship is terminated. We further argue that ghost beliefs and cognitions are probably universal cross-culturally and are common, though unreported, in our own society. We suggest that the pressure of American rationalism on bereaved persons leads them to question their own sanity if they experience ghost cognitions and to keep such cognitions to themselves, thereby increasing the stress of bereavement for those who experience such cognitions. We also document in this chapter the cross-cultural commonality of fear of ghosts and discuss a number of possible explanations for ghost fear. Finally, we show that, as part of normal tie-breaking, people generally believe that over time the distance between the living and ghosts increases.

Chapter 4

Tie-Breaking and
the Death of a Spouse

Of those things which the Abipones do to testify their grief, according to the customs established by their ancestors, some tend to obliterate the memory of the defunct, others to perpetuate it. All the utensils belonging to the lately deceased are burnt on a pile. Besides the horses killed at the tomb, they slay his small cattle if he have any. The house which he inhabited they pull entirely to pieces. His widow, children, and the rest of his family remove elsewhere; and having no house of their own, reside for a time in that of some other person, or lodge miserably under mats. They had rather endure the injuries of the weather, than, contrary to the laws of their countrymen, inhabit a commodious house that has been saddened by the death of the dear master of it. To utter the name of a lately deceased person is reckoned a nefarious offence amongst the Abipones; if, however, occasion requires that mention should be made of that person, they say, "The man that does not now exist," making use of a paraphrase [Dobrizhoffer, *An Account of the Abipones,* 1822: *2,* 273-74].

As we indicated in the preceding chapter, in a long-term relationship such as marriage, innumerable behaviors appropriate to the relationship become associated with stimuli (sights, sounds, odors, textures) in the environment of the relationship. When death (or divorce, or migration, or some other permanent separation) makes it necessary to treat the relationship as ended and to develop new patterns of behavior, these stimuli inhibit the change, because they elicit old dispositions. To facilitate change, tie-breaking practices that eliminate or alter these stimuli seem to be of great value.

We have chosen to focus in this chapter on the relationship of tie-breaking to remarriage of widowed persons, simply because the cross-cultural data on remarriage are much better than the cross-cultural data on the acquisition of other new patterns of behavior following the death of a person with whom one has had a long-term relationship. We do not have a position for or against remarriage following the death of a spouse. We cannot say whether remarriage is desirable or undesirable for any particular widowed person, though even in the United States, where spouses depend on each other relatively little for subsistence (Coppinger and Rosenblatt 1968), it seems that survival chances are reduced when a man becomes widowed (Berardo 1970). This reduction in survival chances could be interpreted as a result of subsistence incompetence, coupled with the psychological and physiological effects of prolonged grief and personal disorganization. Even though remarriage may help to deal with subsistence incompetence and to reduce the psychological and physiological problems that follow the death of a spouse, many widowed persons may find life more comfortable without remarriage or at least without hasty or injudicious movement into a new marriage. The cross-cultural data we report in this chapter should be interpreted as suggesting ways to facilitate remarriage and the assumption of any new or changed pattern of behavior following the death of a spouse, not as suggesting that remarriage is generally a good thing.

The Value of Tie-Breaking Customs

In many societies, there are death customs which eliminate reminders of a deceased spouse during the bereavement period. The excerpt at the beginning of this chapter illustrates many of these customs. The customs include destroying, giving away, or temporarily putting aside personal property of the deceased, observing a taboo on the name of the deceased, and changing residence. We believe that such customs serve to break ties with the deceased spouse and, as a consequence, to facilitate establishment of new patterns of living, including a new marital relationship in which the pattern of interaction, rights, and obligations resembles that in the marriage that was ended by the spouse's death. Such tie-breaking would seem especially useful if the new relationship is between people who formerly had to inhibit marital response to one another, that is between people who formerly knew one another in the stimulus situation associated with the deceased and who did not have a marital type of relationship.

Reminders of a deceased spouse may stimulate responses that are likely to interfere with a new marital or quasi-marital relationship. Consider a widower living in the dwelling he shared with his deceased wife. If activities such as sharing a meal or having sexual relations with some other woman were improper and inhibited in this setting before his wife's death, or even if they were simply not done, they will continue to be more difficult to practice than if the setting were changed. Further, the familiar setting will remind the man of previously well-learned behavior specific to the marriage ended by the death and may even motivate him to engage in such behavior, perhaps a routine morning conversation or a going-to-sleep routine that requires the presence of the deceased wife (see Glick, Weiss, and Parkes 1974: 137, for data on maintenance in a sample of widows in the United States of routines that would be appropriate only if the husband were still alive). When familiar stimuli awaken such residual dispositions, grief may be aroused or intensified, and the acquisition of new responses may be blocked. We believe that spouse-specific response patterns cued by reminders of the spouse occur in all societies. Hence, a common condition of bereavement around the world would seem to be that something resembling marriage to a new person is difficult in the presence of reminders of the previous marriage.

From a cue-conditioning perspective (e.g. Estes 1959; Klinger 1975), the disposition to respond in a manner inconsistent with a new marital relationship would be reduced by elimination of cues to respond as one did while the spouse was still alive and by learning of new responses to the old cues. Thus, discarding or giving away the wife's personal possessions, having others cease using her name in one's presence, or changing feelings about her through fear of her ghost will reduce old response dispositions.

To complicate matters, others in the environment of the widow or widower will retain response dispositions toward the widow or widower which are cued by reminders of the deceased person and which make it difficult for the surviving spouse to enter a new marital routine with someone else. Goldschmidt (1973) provides a poignant example of a Sebei son's reluctance to have his mother remarry. Part of the son's reluctance may well have stemmed from dispositions that were cued by reminders of the deceased. For the son and for others in the environment of the widow, it would be easier to accept a new marital relationship of the widow if reminders of the deceased were reduced. From this discussion of widows and widowers and of others in their environment, it follows that remarriage rates can be expected to be higher in societies where people customarily practice tie-breaking customs.

New Marriages to Old Acquaintances

In many societies, widows tend to remarry according to levirate rules, requiring them to take a new spouse from among men in the kin group of the deceased husband; and in many societies, widowers tend to remarry according to sororate rules, requiring them to take a new spouse from among women in the kin group of the deceased wife. Initially we did not think of the levirate and sororate as likely to require inhibition of previously learned response dispositions. Our naive assumption was that many levirate and sororate arrangements for widows and widowers are with people toward whom sexual and domestic interactions had been marital in spirit. But that does not seem to be a supportable assumption. First of all, many levirate and sororate marriages are with people who may have been outside any category of sexual privilege. Second, reports of actual privileged sexual relations with spouse's biological siblings or with people categorized as siblings by rules of the societal kinship system, "siblings" who would be the prime candidates for a widow or widower to marry by levirate or sororate, are not very common. For example, in Murdock's *Social Structure* (1949: 270) sex relations were rated as freely or conditionally permitted with brother's wife in only thirty-four of 250 societies and with wife's sister in only twenty-eight of 250 societies. By contrast, brother's wife marriage was rated as permitted in 153 societies and sister's husband marriage as permitted in 133 societies. Moreover, even where privileged sex with possible replacement spouse is approved on some occasions, there are ordinarily many occasions when it is inappropriate. Consequently, inhibitions may often be strong even in societies with privileged sex with some potential replacement spouses. Thus, it does not seem very likely that a widowed person marrying by levirate or sororate will have acquired marital response dispositions to the person replacing the deceased spouse. Rather, we would expect, in most cases, a well-learned inhibition of sexuality and domestic interaction. As a consequence, for levirate and sororate remarriage the problems of old response dispositions may be relatively severe. Not only does the couple face the generalized inhibitions of the surviving spouse, but they may also have specific inhibitions to each other. They will have had more likelihood of developing habitual nonmarital patterns of interaction with each other. Furthermore, each may have been learned by the other as a cue to making old responses to the deceased. If so, each could be a cue to grief and to dispositions that block acquisition of a new marital pattern. Thus, tie-breaking customs seem to be even more necessary for sororate and levirate remarriage. This leads to two more hypotheses: (1) Where levirate or sororate remarriage is present, tie-breaking customs are more likely to be present than where levirate or sororate remarriage is absent. (2) There is a stronger relationship between the percentages of remarriage by levirate or sororate and the practice of tie-breaking customs than between the percentages of remarriage not by levirate or sororate and the practice of tie-breaking customs.

The Tie-Breaking Customs Studied

We measured five potential tie-breaking customs: disposal, giving away or putting aside for a substantial amount of time some personal property of the deceased; destruction of useful property of the deceased; temporarily or permanently abandoning the dwelling or a room of the dwelling in which survivors and deceased lived together; temporarily or permanently abandoning the campsite or community in which the survivors lived with the deceased; and the practice of a temporary or permanent taboo on the name of the deceased. The following ethnographic passages illustrate these five practices.

When a person dies, the body is dressed in its best clothes and laid lengthwise by the hearth, the feet toward the doorway, ready for the departure to Hades. Should the deceased be a man, his bow, arrows and quiver, his pipe, tobacco-box, fire sticks and tinder or flint and steel for obtaining light, a long and short knife, a sword, a cup and tray, moustache-lifters and a small bundle of clothes are placed by his side. The clothes are cut or torn and the other things broken or chipped. All these articles are buried with the body. The cutting, chipping and breaking are said to be done in order to kill the things and send their spirits off to heaven with the corpse [Batchelor, *Ainu Life and Lore*, 1927: 155]. [The Ainu are aboriginal people of northern Japan.]

. . . all of the bulk of the portable property of the deceased, such as (in the case of a man) his spears, pots, baskets, paddles, plates and a great variety of other articles, are broken or otherwise rendered unserviceable; and then the whole are conveyed to the cemetery in order to be deposited at the proper time on the grave or at the head-post, this being one of the essential sacrifices prescribed by time-honoured custom [Man, *The Nicobar Islands and Their People*, 1932: 132]. [The Nicobar Islands are in the Bay of Bengal, south of Burma and north of Sumatra.]

The fact of death is established by the cessation of breathing. Shavante then feel for the heart, and, if that has stopped too, they begin to wail, *"moto der,"* they say, meaning "gone dead." The same phrase can also be applied to unconsciousness or any unusually deep sleep and Shavante believe that the soul leaves the body on such occasions. Once the heart has stopped, however, they know that the soul will not return and it is on this account that they start to weep. During the weeping the mourners crouch round the corpse and rarely stir away from it. The possessions of the deceased— his sleeping mat, weapons, and ceremonial ornaments, in the case of a man; her gourds, firefans, carrying-baskets, in the case of a woman—are torn apart or broken in pieces and put onto a big fire which is kindled in front of the hut. . . .
. . . [One] man went to fantastic lengths to obliterate all traces of his deceased wife, for everything that reminded him of her caused him acute sadness. He even set out along the

trail of the last trek on which she had accompanied him and destroyed all the shelters she had built, so that he would not happen upon them later and feel sad [Maybury-Lewis, *Akwĕ-Shavante Society*, 1967: 280-81]. [The Shavante live in Central Brazil.]

Of the deceased's possessions, only those of which he had been particularly fond were buried with him or burned at the potlatch. Other objects were saved as mementoes, to be exhibited at the potlatch. These keepsakes were never used, and were kept hidden from the sight of the relatives, lest the latter should feel sad [Birket-Smith and De Laguna, *The Eyak Indians of the Copper River Delta, Alaska*, 1938: 165].

A widow would burn the things of her husband which were not placed with his body nor taken by his relatives. She would then be smudged with sage. . . .
These practices were seemingly tied up with two beliefs—the first being that if objects were not placed with the body, the deceased would return to look for the things valued in life; the second, that the recently deceased try to lure the living to join them [Flannery, *The Gros Ventres of Montana*, 1953: 203].

Just after the burial, all the inhabitants of the village go to the lake or the river to bathe. The grave-diggers nibble a *ndjao*, the root of a reed which has magical power. Special rites will then be performed for the widows. . . . When they come back from the pool, one of the men climbs on the hut and removes from its top the crown of woven grass, which was its glory during the life of its master. The hut participates in the general state of uncleanness of all his belongings. This crown will be put before the door to close it, and no one will dare to enter any more till the day of the crushing of the hut [Junod, *The Life of a South African Tribe*, 1927: *1*, 144]. [The group described is the Thonga.]

As to speak a dead man's name was a cruel insult, if he had to be mentioned, "deceased" was added at the end. For this reason, when someone died in the village, the chiefs promptly announced the fact in a loud voice through the village, so that he might no longer be named without "the late." If anyone in the same village had the same name as the deceased, he changed it for some time in order not to irritate the wound of the afflicted relatives [Tooker, "An Ethnography of the Huron Indians, 1615-1649," 1964: 134].

There was a taboo on the names of the dead, and especially
on those of dead ancestors. No Toda liked to speak of the
dead by name, but to utter the name of a dead elder relative
was strictly forbidden, and to the end of my visit I never heard
the name of a dead man from one of his descendants. Thus
the last piece of genealogical information which I collected
was that of the names of the father and mother of Kodrner,
my constant attendant. The fact that he was always with me
had prevented my inquiries into his parentage [Rivers, *The
Todas*, 1967: 462]. [The Todas are a tribal people of India.]

Findings

Two of the measures that we attempted to make on widowers,
percentage of widowers remarrying and percentage of widowers
remarrying by the sororate, did not survive methodological
screening (see Appendix, section 4.0). Consequently, we have
one usable measure on widowers (presence vs. absence of remarriage by the sororate), but all three of the measures that
were attempted on widows (percentage remarrying, percentage
remarrying by the levirate, and presence vs. absence of remarriage by the levirate).

All the tendencies in the data are in the same direction. In
general, tie-breaking customs occur where remarriage rates
are higher and where remarriage by the sororate or levirate
is present. The strongest data are for percentage of widows remarrying by the levirate. Where that percentage is high, there
is a strong tendency for personal property of deceased persons
to be disposed of, for useful property to be destroyed, for a
name taboo to be present, for a dwelling or rooms of dwellings
to be abandoned, and for the camp or village to be abandoned.
Percentage of widows remarrying is strongly related to destruction of useful property and to abandonment of the dwelling of
the deceased or of a room of that dwelling. Both the sororate
and the levirate are strongly associated with disposal of personal objects of the deceased and the destruction of useful
property, and there is also a strong relation between presence
of the levirate and presence of a taboo on the name of the
deceased. In general, the data are rather convincing. Where
tie-breaking customs are practiced, i.e. where reminders of
the deceased are eliminated, remarriage rates are higher, and
there is a greater likelihood of the presence of remarriage by

the sororate or levirate. (See Appendix section 4.0 for statistical and methodological details.)

One of the tie-breaking variables, destruction of useful personal property, is strongly related to all four remarriage variables. This tie-breaking variable seems the best candidate for most powerful and most available tie-breaking mechanism. In contrast, temporary or permanent camp or village abandonment is strongly related to only one of the remarriage variables. The difference between the variable that is strongly tied to all four remarriage variables and the variable that is strongly tied to only one remarriage variable is an understandable one. Destroying personal property of somebody else seems an easier behavior to engage in than abandonment of dwelling and living area. Abandonment of dwelling and living area would be costly in terms of effort, economics, and perhaps psychological disruption, especially in societies with difficult-to-build dwellings. In fact, in our sample, societies with relatively permanent walls for typical dwellings (e.g. adobe brick as opposed to woven grass) are less likely to have destruction or abandonment of a dwelling or a part of a dwelling or to have camp or community abandonment following a death. Thus, people are less inclined to break ties by destroying or leaving a dwelling where dwellings are solid and presumably difficult to make and to destroy. Additionally, house destruction or abandonment might inconvenience many people who are not very seriously bereaved. In contrast, destroying the deceased's personal property is considerably easier, in that the property is likely to be duplicated among the possessions of others or else not needed by others. However attractive someone else's garments, tools, and bedding are, they are not likely to be necessary for the survival or even the comfort of others. We realize that the concept of personal property as Americans use it is not present in some societies, but we think that our analysis makes sense for the many societies in which it is present in some form.

An examination of relative frequencies of community abandonment and property destruction indicates that community abandonment is in fact much less popular than property destruction. Our raters judged disposal of personal property of the deceased present in forty-two of fifty societies, whereas community abandonment was rated present in only seven of sixty-two societies. Thus, property destruction seems more serviceable in tie-breaking, because it is a less costly path to follow. Small wonder, then, that it should be so strongly related to remarriage.

All five of the tie-breaking variables are more strongly correlated with percentage of widows remarrying by levirate than with percentage of widows remarrying whether or not by the levirate. This difference supports our hypothesis that tie-breaking is more facilitative of a levirate remarriage than of a nonlevirate remarriage. Where the two people who would marry are both inhibited by reminders of the deceased, and perhaps of well-learned nonmarital responses to each other, removal of the reminders is more facilitative of marriage.

In attempting to understand the role of name taboos, we added an additional measure—a measure of whether the name taboo, if present, "applies primarily to behavior of close relatives of the deceased adult and/or to behavior in the presence of close relatives of the deceased." If a key function of name taboos is to break ties for the spouse or spouses of the deceased, then it seems to us that relatively often name taboos would apply primarily to close kinsmen of the deceased or to people in their presence. In fact, for fourteen of the eighteen societies that we could rate on this variable, this was the case; the name taboo did apply primarily to close relatives or to people speaking in their presence. Moreover, in the case of the four apparently deviant societies, the name taboo seems to have applied to all people in the community, including the close kin. Thus, in all eighteen cases, the name taboo can be thought of as serving the needs of the most bereaved persons in the community.

Deviant Case Analysis: Tie-Breaking and Remarriage

Analysis of deviant cases was instructive in probing the limits of theory in Chapter 2 and Chapter 3. In this chapter, such an analysis is also illuminating. There are seven cases in our sample which (1) lack any tie-breaking custom or have only token disposal or destruction of personal property of the deceased and (2) have levirate or a percentage of remarriage of widows greater that 0 percent. (We lack any deviant cases with sororate remarriage present.) How the deviant cases handle widow remarriage is of interest. By our theory, they should either have some kind of tie-breaking for remarrying widows, or they should have troubled remarriages.

Our seven deviant cases are the Gheg, Kafa, Katab, Koreans, Santal, Tikopia, and Zapotec. One problem in discussing them is that they are not strongly described in the area of tie-breaking. For our five measures of tie-breaking customs, one or both raters could not make a rating on an average of 2.43 items for these seven deviant cases, while the other seventy-one societies in the sample lack reliably ratable information on an average of only 1.21 of the five items. Nonetheless, examination of ethnographic descriptions of widow remarriages in the seven deviant societies is instructive. For five of the seven, widows who remarry change residence, whereas widows who do not remarry usually stay in the residence they were living in before the death of the husband. The five are the Kafa (we infer residence change from Huntingford 1955: 114-15), Katab (Meek 1931: 2, 37), Koreans (Brandt 1971: 132), Tikopia (Firth 1936: 175), and Zapotec (Parsons 1936: 68). The Brandt reference we cite for the Koreans is not a source that was used in making ratings in this study; however, the source of our extracts, Osgood (1951), was unclear about residence for remarrying widows. We thought it safe to use Brandt, because on points that both Osgood and Brandt discussed there was considerable overlap.

Of the remaining two cases, we lack residence data on the Santal, where at any rate remarriage rates are very low (Culshaw 1949: 146). For the Gheg of Albania, widow remarriages, which are usually leviratic, ordinarily do not involve change in residence. As our theory would lead us to expect, Gheg remarriages are often seriously troubled (Durham 1928: 171). There are even reports of remarried Gheg widows running away. Although Durham's discussion suggests that a principal source of the problem for the society is lack of freedom of choice for widows, it may well be that underlying the freedom of choice problem is a deficiency in tie-breaking. If the widows had a choice, they would choose to marry away from the inhibiting cues of home and husband's brother. But if tie-breaking customs were practiced, perhaps Gheg widows would not feel so strongly so often that they would rather marry someone other than husband's brother and that they would rather move, on remarriage, to another residence.

Our deviant case analysis has augmented our theorizing by suggesting that change in residence for remarrying widows is a functional alternative to other means of tie-breaking. The epistemological status of residence change as a tie-breaking custom is, of course, low, because residence change was first identified as tie-breaking in a post hoc explanation of deviant cases. However, residence change fits our theoretical conception of what is necessary for a custom to be tie-breaking, involving, as it does, a change from the stimulus setting of the marriage ended by death. Further, the one deviant case for which residence change does not occur is the one deviant for which there are reports of troubled remarriages.

Alternative Interpretations

One possible alternative interpretation of the relationship of tie-breaking customs to remarriage is that the destruction of property and the abandonment of dwelling increase the dependency needs of surviving spouses. With home and subsistence-getting tools lost, remarriage is more necessary and desirable. There are, however, some deficiencies in this alternative. One is that it cannot account for the results involving name taboo. Another is that there are many alternatives to marriage that would meet dependency needs, i.e. returning to consanguineal kin, taking up residence with same-sex unmarrieds, or becoming dependent on spouse's kin but without a marital relationship.

Another alternative interpretation is that remarriage causes dwelling and property loss, rather than the reverse being the case. One could argue that once a person remarries there is not a need to maintain the former dwelling or to use the property formerly used. However, this alternative explanation also does not account for the data on name taboo, and it is clear from many of our cases that dwelling and property loss typically antecede remarriage rather than follow it.

Ghost Fear and Remarriage

The presence of ghost fear is strongly related to the percentage of widows who remarry and to the other three remarriage variables. In general, where ghost fear is present, remarriage rates are great and the levirate and sororate are more likely to be present. The fear of ghosts is not strongly associated with the tie-breaking variables, so its relationship to remarriage does not seem to be a result of its somehow motivating tie-breaking. Rather, there seems a direct linkage of ghost fear to remarriage. Apparently ghost fear provides a tie-breaking, not through elimination of reminders of the deceased, but through altering the image of the deceased. As was suggested in the preceding chapter, ghost fear may lead the bereaved to think of the deceased as something fearful in ways that motivate cutting ties with the deceased. The fear may motivate people to engage both in ceremonial acts and in thought processes that free them from their ties to the deceased. However, the only clear relationship in our data that would back up that speculation is a relationship between degree of ghost fear and ceremonial cleansing of widows; where ghost fear is greater, there is more likely to be ceremonial cleansing of a widow in order to remove symbolically (or actually, depending on one's view of reality) her linkage with her deceased husband. It would be useful to have direct data on the relationship of ghost fear to alteration of the bereaved's image of the deceased and to elimination of behavioral dispositions that were appropriate while the deceased was alive. But we do not have such data, so our thoughts about the effect of ghost fear remain speculative. It would be difficult to find such data in the cross-cultural literature, but perhaps a study of fear of ex-spouse and adjustment to divorce among Americans would get at the same mechanisms. If we are right about the role of ghost fear, and if the analogy between fear of the ghost of deceased spouse and fear of divorced ex-spouse is adequate, then divorced people who fear the ex-spouse should be found to break more quickly their psychological ties with the ex-spouse and to acquire more quickly patterns of behavior inconsistent with those engaged in during the former marriage.

Tie-Breaking and Other Theoretical Perspectives

Benedict (1938) argued that if people have to change over the life cycle from one well-learned and important pattern of behavior to another that is quite different, a change which she labeled a "discontinuity in cultural conditioning," the times of change will be times of difficulty. For example if children in their teens have to change from being dependent to being autonomous, the teen years will, she argued, be a time of stress. Our data and theory concerning tie-breaking would suggest, however, that changes bring much less serious problems when the stimulus situation changes. If changes must be made in adolescence from being dependent to being independent, stress could be minimized by a simultaneous change in stimulus situation— for example a move to another residence, a marked decrease in contacts with people who were important while one was dependent, or a change in one's own name. Remarrying, acquiring a new parent, or fostering a child to replace one who has died could conceivably involve "discontinuity in cultural conditioning," but the stress of the change will be minimal if there is an accompanying change in the stimulus situation.

Theories dealing with working through of grief might argue that tie-breaking activities could arrest or postpone needed working through. Practicing a taboo on the name of the deceased, for example, might prolong one's grief by delaying one's coming to grips with the reality of the death. We would argue, however, that a reduction in reminders of the deceased can aid working through by reducing the amount of old learning that has to be unlearned.

Mandler (1964) has pointed out that a death of somebody with whom one has had substantial contact removes an important stimulus in one's life, so that part of the emotional load of grief is the anxiety that comes from missing a stimulus and, consequently, not knowing what to do. Mandler might argue, for example, that a widow will experience distress at suppertime and going-to-bed time, because the absence of the familiar stimulus, the spouse, blocks the old pattern of behavior and makes it difficult to do anything in the situation. We agree with Mandler, but argue that the familiar stimuli still present set off old response patterns. Thus, at times bereavement in the old stimulus situation may involve ambivalence or response conflict (cf. Klinger 1975), at times it may involve an insufficiency of response dispositions, and at times it may involve problems stemming from dispositions that are no longer appropriate.

Jensen and Wallace (1967) have pointed to some of the difficulties that can arise in a family when the death of a family member makes it necessary that family members learn new responses to each other, when the survivors try to reorganize their own relationships in order to fill the gap created by the death. Children, for example, may demand more time than before from a surviving parent and may require the surviving parent to act in new ways—exercising authority in ways not done before, for example. As a consequence, part of the difficulty people experience during bereavement may stem from frustrated attempts to have other family members take the place of the deceased person and from the pain of learning to respond in new ways in order to meet the needs of other surviving family members. These difficulties seem almost inevitable in such a situation, in part because each person in the family is a stimulus to patterns of behavior that were appropriate before the death but that are no longer appropriate. However, a change in stimulus context for the interactions will eliminate some of the cues to the old patterns of behavior and make it easier to change.

Applications to the United States

Our results suggest that remarriage in the United States could be facilitated by customary disposal of the personal property of the deceased, customary change of residence, and customary name taboo. (It seems unlikely that fear of ghost could become customary.) Spouses who move, who reduce the frequency with which they mention the name of the deceased spouse, who rid themselves of personal possessions of the deceased spouse and of other reminders of the deceased spouse would probably find it easier to establish new marital or quasi-marital relationships. Corroborative data come from Gorer (1965: 85-87), who reports that among the people he had studied who had done

the poorest working through of grief were six who were purposely keeping the possessions of the deceased and the arrangement of household furnishings as they were before the death
to serve as a kind of memorial to the deceased.

Children are a problem from the point of view of tie-breaking.
If a surviving spouse lives with his or her children, they may,
as our discussion earlier in this chapter suggests, be a very
strong reminder of the deceased spouse. Furthermore, children
may themselves exert direct pressure against remarriage. This
seems to have been the case in Parkes' study of twenty-two
London widows (1970, 1972: 100). Remarriage might be delayed in cases where children are present, perhaps until the
last child moves away from home. However, the issues are not
simple. Children may satisfy some needs so that there is less
need for a replacement for the deceased spouse, but they may
also create additional need for a spouse who can be a helpmate
and an ally in coping with children.

In Parkes' studies (1970, 1972), fourteen of the twenty-two
widows reported avoidance of reminders of the deceased
husband. Included in avoidance behavior were avoidance
of a bed, staying out of rooms, and getting rid of possessions.
Similar data come from Hobson (1964), Marris (1958), and
Yamamoto et al. (1969). Thus, bereaved people may often
have dispositions to avoid reminders of the deceased, even
in cultures that lack customs for eliminating such reminders.
Nonetheless, we believe that making tie-breaking customary
is far more effective than leaving surviving spouses on their
own. Without the force of custom to engage in the tie-breaking
acts, any acts that eliminate reminders of the deceased may
seem to be disrespectful to the dead, selfish, or frivolous. Some
of these acts may be economically costly, which would increase reluctance to engage in them. Moreover, there are
likely to be countervailing attractions from the reminders; they
may, for example, be sources of pleasant or identity-relevant
memories (cf. Townsend 1963: 38-39). Thus, the tie-breaking
acts are potentially of value, but are not as likely to be used by
many if they are left as mere options advocated by counselors
and the popular literature on dealing with bereavement.
Custom simplifies life by making difficult decisions unnecessary.

We would expect the residues of ties to be present for people other than the spouse. In a work setting, for example, long-term coworkers would have old dispositions to deal with when faced with a replacement for a deceased coworker. The children of a deceased person would be inhibited by reminders of the deceased parent from treating a step-parent as a parent. For these people, too, tie-breaking would seem helpful.

In applying the findings of this chapter, one must keep in mind that many people who have moved soon after the death of a spouse or other person with whom they have had an important coresidential relationship have subsequently come to regret the move. This is not to say that they failed to benefit in the short run from the move. The loss of reminders of the deceased may well have facilitated assuming new, adaptive patterns of behavior. However, the move may in the long run prove to be costly. As Fried (1963) has argued, losing a residence may itself be bereaving.

Some possible costs of a move are obvious—the expense, the effort, and the possibility of increasing the distance one lives from important places, such as the homes of friends and valued relatives, work, preferred shopping places, and schools. Then, too, a bereaved person may, while eliminating inhibiting and distressing reminders of the deceased, eliminate reminders of things it would be better to retain—dispositions that are an important part of the self and pleasant or significant memories. For example in moving to a different residence, a widow may make it more difficult to retain memories of her children growing up and the good times she had with her husband, and she may lose a garden, a work area, or a favorite nook for reading that helped her to be herself. Habenstein (1968) has written about the "impoverishment of self" one experiences at the death of an intimate. One loses the chats, arguments, memory-sharing, coordinated life routine, support for one's values, and self-identity that were all provided by the other person. Thus, at the death of someone important, it is an especially great threat to one's self-concept to discard other things of the self by moving. Perhaps some people can benefit from an opportunity to change self-concept, but it is likely that the exigencies of bereavement may motivate some bereaved people to eliminate stimuli to the self-concept that they will, after the exigencies have dissipated, regret having eliminated.

Perhaps a wiser change with regard to one's dwelling would be to maintain the dwelling while altering it—redecorating, moving furniture, changing the uses of some of the rooms. This would enable one to retain some of the stimuli to self and to memories worth keeping, while facilitating the acquisition of new patterns of behavior.

For people thinking of getting rid of possessions, such as old furniture or tools and garments of the deceased, the same risks exist of grief over loss of the possessions and of threat to self-concept and memories. Even though the change in stimuli if one got rid of some possessions might facilitate acquiring new patterns of behavior and reduce the duration of the grief felt for the lost person, the net change might be to greater grief. Thus, it might be wise to delay getting rid of possessions until the grief is at least partly worked through. Perhaps putting possessions of the deceased in an out-of-the-way part of the dwelling would be a useful compromise between getting rid of them completely and having them around as deterrents to changing behavior patterns. It may even be possible to use the discarding of the possessions of the deceased some months after the death as a symbolic end of one's mourning. As we discuss at length in the next chapter, such formal ends to mourning are quite common cross-culturally and are apparently quite useful.

Of course for people who have not been employed outside the home, another way of changing the stimulus situation while retaining some of the valued aspects of a dwelling and of things in the dwelling is to go to work. This puts one in a novel stimulus situation enough of the time that some new learning can be facilitated. It does not do away with the pain and difficulty one might experience when returning home, but it may develop new contacts and new interests which would speed up acquiring new responses in the old situation.

The stimulus analysis of grief would not be complete without our pointing to some factors that guarantee that stimuli to grief and to old response dispositions cannot be dispelled completely or quickly when a close social relationship is terminated. Some of the stimuli to old response dispositions are inside of one; they cannot be escaped. Feelings of sexual desire, of hunger, of fatigue, of sickness, and so on may all cue response dispositions that would only be appropriate if the deceased were still alive. Furthermore, over the calendrical cycle new stimuli to the old ways emerge inescapably—an anniversary date, the Christmas season, the first snowfall of the year, tulips in spring, the due date for income tax returns, the beginning of the baseball season, and so on (cf. Glick, Weiss, and Parkes 1974: 150). Bereaved persons can be expected to be confronted again and again with stimuli that set off grief feelings and old response dispositions.

Chapter Summary

In this chapter we argue that tie-breaking customs which separate one from reminders of a deceased spouse facilitate remarriage. These tie-breaking customs include discarding or temporarily putting out of sight personal property of the deceased, practicing a taboo on the name of the deceased, and changing residence. Applications of these findings to the situation of bereaved persons in the United States are discussed. In general, it seems that the acquisition of new behavior patterns is promoted by elimination of stimuli to the old patterns, but that the elimination of any familiar stimuli risks adding to one's grief. Additional findings were reported that indicate that tie-breaking customs are especially facilitative of remarriage to a person one knew before the spouse's death and that ghost fear, which may motivate cognitive transformations or ceremonial behaviors that cut psychological ties with the deceased, also facilitates remarriage.

Chapter 5

Ceremonies

> Before sitting down to the meal, the assembly prays in unison for the soul of the deceased. One of the relatives eulogizes the deceased by emphasizing the good qualities of his personality. When this obligation is completed, the affair takes on a different aspect. The mood is gay and may even become quite ribald. At a minimum, conversation is lively and there is joking and laughter. This may be the first family gathering in several years, and everyone is interested in catching up on family news [Douglass, *Death in Murelaga*, 1969: 47]. [Murelaga is a Spanish Basque village.]

For many of the world's peoples, death ceremonies commonly occur over a substantial period of time after a death. These ceremonies may take place weeks, months, a year, or more beyond the time of a death, and they often involve reburial or some other attention to the remains of the deceased.

Functions of Any Ceremony

It seems common that death ceremonies serve valuable functions having nothing directly to do with grief, mourning, allocation of inheritance, or any other problem resulting from a death. In fact, any life cycle or calendrical ceremony serves valuable functions with no direct connection to the event being marked. Ceremonies of any sort may serve to renew ties and reinforce them (cf. Hickerson 1960), to provide an opportunity for marriages and other alliances to be established, to entertain, to promote exchanges of valuables, to remind people of obligations, to enable people to test whom they can trust and whom they cannot, to transmit news, to transmit information of survival value, to increase intake of animal protein, and to accomplish many other things. It would be gross oversimplification to discuss death ceremonies without noting this vast range of functions not directly resulting from needs created by a death that death ceremonies may serve.

Death Ceremonies as Ceremonies of Passage

Death ceremonies can be thought of as rites of passage (van Gennep 1960). Rites of passage include some kind of disconnection with an inital status and role, a liminal or in-between period, and the incorporation into a new status and role. Van Gennep and others have pointed out that in societies throughout the world, death is followed by passage ceremonies for the deceased—who must be removed from the world of the living to the symbolic world of the dead—and for the immediate survivors—who must be removed from statuses and roles lost when the death occurred (e.g. from the status and role of being a spouse or from the status and role of being somebody's offspring) and incorporated into new statuses and roles, such as head of a family.

A crucial process going on in passage is one of commitment (Rosenblatt 1974a; Rosenblatt, Fugita, and McDowell 1969; Rosenblatt and Unangst 1974). By commitment, we mean a process of binding oneself with minimum reservations to certain statuses, roles, attitudes, plans, activities, understandings, perceptions, and beliefs. The living must be psychologically committed to passage from old conditions to new ones. But obtaining such commitment is not simple. As was indicated in the previous two chapters, bereaved people retain many strong dispositions that were appropriate before the death occurred. These dispositions cannot be altered or terminated easily or abruptly (cf. Marris 1974). Hence, the committing process must be a powerful one and must involve a substantial amount of time.

Theories dealing with commitment (Brehm and Cohen 1962; Kiesler 1971; Rosenblatt 1974a; Rosenblatt and Unangst

1974) tell us that commitments are greater when they are public rather than private, voluntary rather than involuntary, and effortful rather than easy. People familiar with Festinger's theory of cognitive dissonance (1957) will recognize that these elements of strongly committing situations maximize cognitive dissonance pressures to drop old dispositions and take on new ones. People familiar with self-perception theory (Bem 1972) will recognize that behavior that is voluntary, effortful, and public is likely to produce a self-perception that one is a person who has strong internal dispositions in support of the behavior. Thus, a person at a funeral who voluntarily engages in some effortful acts that indicate acceptance of the death (such as pallbearing or shoveling dirt onto the newly interred coffin) would find it dissonant or inconsistent with self-perceptions to behave in the future as though the death had not occurred and would be inclined to perceive self as accepting of the death.

One gain from having death ceremonies well attended is that heavy attendance provides the publicity that is one of the conditions for strong commitment to acceptance of the fact of a death. In our data on attendance at funeral ceremonies for deceased adults, the number of people at initial ceremonies is judged by our raters to exceed twenty-five in 94 percent of sixty-eight ratable societies, and attendance at final ceremonies is judged to exceed twenty-five in 84 percent of thirty-two ratable societies. Thus, it seems that a substantial group of witnesses is available at times when the typical bereaved adult somewhere in the world has an opportunity to engage in acts indicating acceptance of a death.

In the performance of acts of mourning it seems important, from the point of view of the psychology of commitment, that bereaved persons believe that they are performing their mourning acts because they want to, not because they are being forced by others. But what of societies in which every bereaved person adheres to mourning norms? Is there any freedom of choice in such societies? Even in societies where norms of mourning are obeyed by all bereaved persons, feelings of volition may be present for all mourners. One need only feel a desire to do the right thing or a desire to express one's feelings of grief in a way that others may understand in order to feel substantial freedom of choice in performance of mourning acts.

Effort in mourning may well be present in all societies. The act of participating in the disposal of the body of someone important to one may itself require enormous psychological effort. The emotional draining in expressing grief, the difficulty in going through a complex ceremony, expenditures of energy and resources in the carrying out of the ceremony, the possible abandonment of dwelling, the changes in habitual ways of doing things, and so on are surely all substantial efforts in the direction of committing one to accepting the fact of a death. And the feelings of intrapersonal conflict when old dispositions compete with the changes one is attempting in one's behavior are surely effort enough to guarantee commitment to the new dispositions one eventually acquires.

Thus, in terms of publicity, volition, and effort, death ceremonies may be quite effective at committing people to accept the fact of a death, to drop no longer appropriate statuses and roles, to take on the status and role of a mourner, and eventually to assume new statuses and roles. However, the process is not one that can occur quickly and easily. The old dispositions cannot be dropped abruptly, even if many of the visual and auditory cues to the old dispositions have been removed or altered. For societies in our sample that were measurable on mourning duration for one or more category of bereaved person, the average mourning period for widowers was 215 days, for widows 305 days, and for bereaved adult offspring of the deceased 193 days. As we indicate in the Appendix, these means are approximations. Nonetheless it seems clear that societies typically provide a substantial amount of time for people who were closely tied to a deceased adult to work through their emotional reactions and conflicts over the death and over becoming committed to the new statuses and roles they must assume following the death. However, the mere passage of time does not guarantee change and commitment to change. This can be seen upon examination of the functions of final funeral ceremonies occurring weeks, months, a year, or more after a death.

Time-Limiting Function of Final Ceremonies

Gorer (1965), Hertz (1960), and Lafitau (1724) have asserted that one function of final ceremonies is to put a time limit on the bereavement period. By having a well-defined and substantial time during which mourning norms allow or coerce expressions of grief, feelings may be vented, and the process of working through can occur. Working through may well be facilitated by anticipation of a final ceremony. Where a final ceremony is to occur, the bereaved person goes through the mourning period knowing that there will be a point at which the expressions of feelings are expected to end. As a consequence, during the time leading up to the final ceremony, the bereaved is likely to be going through psychological preparation for the postmourning period. At the final cermony, the bereaved becomes publicly committed to finish with mourning. Often the commitment involves the dropping of symbols of mourning. At this time, too, the people who are important in the life of the bereaved become committed to accepting the end of mourning of the bereaved. This last is important, because often prolonged mourning is encouraged or seems to be encouraged by people around the bereaved (cf. Lopata 1973: 54, writing about widows in America). Commitment in a final ceremony seems especially valuable, because there are numerous reasons (e.g. guilt, residues of old dispositions, fear of the new) why one might be reluctant, no matter how long the time since a death, to assume the new statuses and roles. Final ceremonies thus seem of value in preventing the prolongation of grief. Consequently, we predicted that societies with final ceremonies would lack prolonged expressions of grief, whereas societies without final ceremonies would have prolonged expressions of grief.

The first two of the following three passages illustrate final ceremonies; the third passage provides an illustration of prolonged grief.

> After a hundred and thirty days a widow comes out of mourning. That night she does not sleep, there is drumming on calabashes until the morning. The morning comes and she bathes herself, she dresses in a new blouse, a new cloth, a new head-kerchief. She takes off her old clothes and gives them as

alms to an old woman. Everyone in your kin and in your husband's kin comes with alms—guineacorn, rice, millet, money. You prepare porridge and *cuge*, the *malams* come and recite the prayers, and you distribute food to them and send it round the compounds. At Azahar everyone who has come for the prayers and greetings gets up and goes home. If the woman is young, not an old lady like me, that same day that the *malams* have recited the last prayers they also recite the marriage verses and she is married again. As I was old I went to the compound of my younger brother Kadiri. . . . [Smith, *Baba of Karo: A Woman of the Muslim Hausa*, 1954: 217]. [The Hausa are concentrated in Northern Nigeria.]

For about two or three months after the death of a spouse or parent, a bereaved man or woman refrained from eating meat, from washing more than the hands, and from participating in social activities. In the case of a spouse's bereavement the family of the deceased decided when the tabus should be lifted; that is, the relatives-in-law provided for a small cleansing ritual and set the date for it. . . .

On the day set the relatives-in-law, headed by one of their group, brought meat and clothing. With them came two or three singers. . . . The singers performed morning and evening, and the chief mourner, his relatives, and any others of his tribe who wished all wept in accompaniment. This performance . . . continued all night. . . .

The next morning . . . the visitors washed the faces of the chief mourners, combed their hair, and dressed them in new clothes. . . . Thereafter the faces of less closely related mourners —cousins, aunts, grandparents, etc.—were washed.

Then a general feast was held, games were played, and one or two shamans might dance during the evening. . . .

Thereafter the initial phase of mourning was over. A widower was free to remarry, though many men did not do so at once. A widow was expected to remain single for at least a year. Any deeply bereaved person continued to maintain a depressed demeanor and refrained from meat until the annual mourning celebration was held [Gayton, "Yokuts and Western Mono Ethnography," 1948: 107-08]. [The Yokuts and Western Mono are California native American groups.]

Long after the death those among the bereaved who really feel a sense of loss will wail whenever they come to think of the departed. This is a spontaneous emotional release, although it is expressed through the same type of wailing as is customary in ceremonial situations. Anything which reminds a Shavante of a lost relative may provoke demonstrations of grief for years after his or her death. One woman always wailed when she heard an aeroplane because there had been one passing over when her husband died [Maybury-Lewis, *Akwē-Shavante Society*, 1967: 281]. [The Shavante live in central Brazil.]

Final Ceremonies: Incidence and Attributes

We defined a final ceremony as a "formal ritual where the recently deceased receives special remembrance and attention. By our definition, it occurs ten days or more after the initial ceremony or ceremonies. In general, the final funeral ceremony is public . . . and formalized." Of the sixty-one societies in our sample that could be assessed on presence or absence of final ceremonies, forty-six (75 percent) were judged to have final funeral ceremonies. From the point of view of Americans, most of whom have only familiarity with an initial funeral ceremony (Bowman 1959: 11), it is remarkable that so many societies have final ceremonies. It suggests that final ceremonies may serve important functions that may not be adequately served for bereaved Americans. However, before going into the discussion of the time-limiting function of final ceremonies, we would like to develop further the concept of final ceremony by discussing data on some common attributes of final ceremonies.

Twenty-nine societies that had final ceremonies could be rated on whether or not there was a series of final ceremonies, with at least one nonceremonial period of at least a week interspersed between ceremonial events. Fifteen (52 percent) of the twenty-nine were judged to have a series of final ceremonies.

Thirty societies with final ceremonies could be rated on whether the final ceremony coincides with annual mortuary ceremonies or with annual feasts which celebrate or worship all deceased from the community or a large number of deceased. The raters were instructed not to count an annual ceremony as a final ceremony unless the recently deceased "receives individual remembrance and attention at the first annual ceremony occurring after his death. This attention must be more elaborate at the first annual mortuary ceremony than it is at any subsequent annual ceremony." In four (13 percent) of the thirty societies that could be rated, final ceremonies were judged to coincide with annual mortuary ceremonies or annual feasts.

In nine (28 percent) of thirty-two societies with final ceremonies, final disposal of the remains of the deceased was judged to occur at the final ceremony. This includes giving the body, bones, or ashes a final resting place or manipulating the remains in some way for the final time. Clearly, reburial or other final disposal of the remains is not a universal attribute of final death ceremonies.

In eighteen (67 percent) of twenty-seven societies with final ceremonies, the final ceremony was judged to terminate mourning. In other words, in two-thirds of the measurable cases, the final ceremony was expected to end the required expressions of grief.

Prolongation of Grief

We attempted to measure specific expressions of grief beyond the end of the mourning period, such things as disrupted work, troubled dreams, suicidal behavior, lamentations uncoerced by any norm, and mental and physical illness as a reaction to a death. But no specific measure could be made on many cases, so a global indicator of grief after the end of mourning was devised that incorporated all the specific indicators.

Findings

The presence of final ceremonies was strongly associated with the global measure of grief after the end of mourning. Where final ceremonies were present, prolonged grief was less likely to be present or frequent; where final ceremonies were absent, prolonged grief was more likely to be present and frequent. Thus, as hypothesized, final ceremonies seem to serve the function of time-limiting grief.

Although it seems plausible to us that final ceremonies promote adjustment through the generation of commitment to end mourning, there is an alternative interpretation of the correlation between presence of final ceremonies and grief after the end of mourning that must be considered. Final ceremonies may be associated with longer mourning durations. If so, it may not be that final ceremonies help to terminate grief but that they are merely a sign that mourning duration is long. If this were so, the association of grief after the end of mourning with absence of final ceremonies might be due to mourning duration being too short where final ceremonies are absent. Final ceremonies, however, have no statistical relation to mourning duration. Thus the relation between grief after the end of mourning and final ceremonies is not an artifact of the relation of mourning duration to prolongation of grief.

Ceremony Attendance and Time-Limiting of Grief

Time-limiting of mourning seems useful in ending grief, and, as the data presented above suggest, final ceremonies seem often to end the mourning period and to curtail effectively expressions of grief. But as we indicated earlier in this chapter, a mere rule of time-limiting or a mere commemorative event, without public commitment by a bereaved person and by others important in the bereaved person's social environment, seems insufficient to terminate grief. In our data there is a suggestive finding in support of this position. It is based on few cases. In societies with final funeral ceremonies, grief after the end of mourning is less likely to occur, the heavier the attendance at the final ceremony. (See Appendix section 5.0 for technical details.)

Attendance Inducements

People other than the most bereaved may have reasons not to attend funeral ceremonies. It may be inconvenient because of the distance to travel or the weather; the press of such other activities as planting, harvesting, or attending market day; or the burden of gift-giving or assistance-giving. It may be repulsive or frightening because of attitudes toward corpses or because of ghost fears.

However reluctant people are to attend death ceremonies, it still is useful that many do so. They can provide assistance and support to the most bereaved. Their presence enables their relations with the most bereaved to be redefined in light of the death. They can become committed to accepting the death and to the new role assignments and obligations that follow the death, and their presence provides the publicity that facilitates the commitment of other people. Of course, their attendance also provides them and other attenders with the benefits of all ceremonies, such as renewal of ties and transmission of news.

Because people may be reluctant to attend ceremonies, and because their attendance may be of value, we expected that societies would have institutionalized inducements to attend ceremonies. Inducements, as we defined them, would be additional sources of motivation to attend a ceremony—a source of pleasure for attending or a source of pain for not attending. We speculated that at death ceremonies these inducements might include feasting, gaming, dancing, sexual liberties, provision of alcoholic drink, and (at final ceremonies) the holding of a single ceremony for several deceased persons. We measured all of these hypothetical inducements. Of course, any specific inducement might serve additional functions, but we thought all could be important in promoting attendance.

We examined the association of each inducement with an index of the proportion of local group in attendance at initial and final ceremonies for adult dead. Of the eleven inducements, only two are associated with attendance, both with attendance at final ceremonies—holding ceremonies for more than one death at a time and sex liberties (such as an orgy) at final ceremonies. Both correlations are based on such a small number of cases that they must be interpreted with extreme caution.

It seems reasonable to expect that inducements might make the greatest difference in societies with deterrents to attend ceremonies. To explore further the possible usefulness of inducements to attend ceremonies we set out to examine the relationship between inducements and our indexes of proportion of local group attending ceremonies in societies with ghost fear and with body fear. Ghost fear seems a deterrent to attend both initial and final ceremonies, body fear a deterrent to attend at least initial ceremonies. Both fears might well lead people to want to stay away from a corpse, the site of a death, or bereaved persons. Unfortunately, unratable cases on our indexes of attendance, in our measures of inducements, and in our measures of fear combine to make for such small numbers of cases in analyses that the data are simply not strong enough to be worth discussing. Nonetheless, the ideas seem worth noting as guides to future research and thought dealing with death ceremonies.

On Death Ceremonies in the United States

Death ceremonies in the United States seem to be multifunctional, as they are in other societies. In the United States, as elsewhere, they provide opportunities to renew bonds and transmit news and opportunities to redefine relations with others in attendance and for everybody to become publicly committed to accepting the fact of death. However, because many kin functions are carried out by other institutions in the United States, and because there is usually only an initial death ceremony, the importance of death ceremonies in carrying out most functions is probably much less in the United States than elsewhere. Generalizing from the cross-cultural data, however, the real loss in the United States may be the loss of time-limiting of mourning and hence of grief that comes from final ceremonies. Data are needed on American funeral customs. In some ethnic groups, for example, stone-dedication may function as a final ceremony, and orthodox Jews in the United States, as in England (Gorer 1965: 75-83), can be presumed to practice time-limiting of mourning and, hence, of grief. Nonetheless, it seems likely that most bereaved Americans do not experience time-limiting of mourning and grief and, as a consequence, many Americans may experience prolonged grief.

Perhaps this provides some understanding of why remarriage rates are higher for divorcées in the United States than for the widowed, even when age is held constant (Carter, Glick, and Lewit 1955). The final ceremony aspects of divorce decrees may, in some respects, make divorce in the

United States easier than widowhood. Immediate kinsmen and acquaintances will be made aware of a divorce decree, and spouses so parted are publicly defined as free to seek new relationships with people of the opposite sex. The decree is, moreover, like a final ceremony, in that it is preceded by a substantial period of time of adjustment to and anticipation of the formal ending of the relationship. For the widowed person in America or Britain, where mourning is not ended by a final ceremony, remarriage may be delayed out of fear of seeming disloyal to the deceased spouse (Marris 1958: chap. 3). Especially for widowed persons who lack friends and relatives to reassure them that they have satisfactorily displayed their loyalty or love, remarriage may be difficult (Marris 1958: 39-40).

Why Americans generally lack final ceremonies is a matter for speculation. It may be that American death practices in general are overwhelmingly influenced by the desire of the bereaved not to make trouble for others—not to make trouble by being emotional, asking for help, or involving others in ceremony (cf. Gorer 1965). Americans may ordinarily feel that they are supposed to solve their own problems, rather than burden others with them. Whether or not these are, in fact, major factors underlying the lack of final ceremonies in America, it is our guess that unless Americans are willing to recognize that at times they must burden other people and turn to others for help, it will be difficult to institutionalize final ceremonies here.

Chapter Summary

The major contribution of this chapter to thinking about grief and mourning is the development of theory and documentation concerning the role of final funeral ceremonies, generally occurring weeks or months after a death, in the effective termination of bereavement. In societies without final funeral ceremonies, there is more likely to be prolonged grief. The obvious application of this finding to bereavement in the United States is discussed. Also discussed in this chapter are inducements to attend ceremonies, the role of heavy attendance in achieving commitment to a new state of affairs, the functions of all ceremonies, and death ceremonies as rites of passage and commitment.

Part 3.

Concluding Section

This section of the book begins with a discussion of a complex of culture traits that occurs commonly throughout the world—Christianity. If we are to use the findings of our research to provide a cross-cultural perspective on grief and mourning in America, it seems important to know how Christianity is related to grief and mourning in other cultures. As we report in Chapter 6, we find that Christianity has few noticeable relationships to our measures of grief, mourning, and death customs. That finding makes us much more confident that our suggestions in the previous chapters about grief and mourning in America have some validity. There seem to be relatively few constraints on the mourning customs of a society as a result of Christianity being important in the society, and the dynamics of grief and mourning do not seem to be related to variations in the importance of Christianity.

Although we find that Christianity seems to have little relationship to grief, mourning, and death customs, we find it in some interesting patterns of relationship involving widows, women in general, and the treatment of property. It is not so much on exotic customs that Christianity has its effects as on the supply of and demand for wives and on the fate of the property of a deceased person.

In Chapter 7, we provide further perspective on American customs and experiences. In it we discuss, from the perspective of our theory and findings, commonly recommended ways of dealing with grief in America (i.e. drugs, catharsis of emotion, and prompt return to daily routines), education for grief and mourning for losses other than a death, and future research needs.

Chapter 6

The Effect of
Christianity on Death Customs

In order to evaluate grief and mourning in America, it seems necessary to put American Christianity in perspective. Christianity is the religion of the large majority of Americans. How much is Christianity a factor that must be taken into consideration in understanding grief and mourning in other societies and in assessing American practices and the possibilities for their alteration?

Christianity is present in some form among at least some people in many cultures. For some cultures in our sample, Christianity is present to the same extent and in much the same forms as it is in the United States. In other cultures, it is the religion of a minority. It may be amalgamated with non-Christian religious beliefs, or it may be present as one of several religious systems competing for the allegiances of an educated elite or of all the people of a society. In many other cultures, there has been no impact of Christianity. These variations in the degree of Christian influence enable us to estimate some of the effects of Christianity on customs of grief and mourning. It is, of course, always possible that any apparent effect of Christianity is due to the cultural institutions that frequently accompany Christianity—for example a market economy, a European or American legal system, or an increasing variety of consumer goods. But it still seems of value to attempt to assess the impact of Christianity on the variables we have been studying.

Christianity is associated in our sample with larger communities and with the importance of animal husbandry
and agriculture in providing calories. Our inclination is to
believe both that Christianity arrives at a society with larger
communities and with agriculture and/or animal husbandry
because such settings are more congenial to colonial ex-
ploitation and to missionaries, and that Christianity is accompanied by economic institutions that promote population
concentration and an increase in the importance of agriculture and animal husbandry as sources of calories.

When we turn to our data on the influence of Christianity
on death customs, we find that Christianity has surprisingly
little effect. It seems to reduce reincarnation beliefs, but it
seems to have almost no direct influence on ceremonies or
ceremonialism, beliefs about spirits, fear of body, or body
disposal procedures. And Christianity fails with remarkable
consistency to be related to the other aspects of culture we
have studied. One would assume that a change in religion
would affect all ceremony, all beliefs about spirits, attitudes
toward corpses, and funeral practices. Why Christianity
does not have such an impact is a subject for speculation.
It seems possible that Christian missionaries do not advocate
change in all the elements of culture that might be called
religious. Instead, they may push only for acceptance of
some doctrine and for the ending of a few practices. In fact,
it may even be important to the success of a mission that
it not fight most aspects of indigenous religious beliefs and
practices. If it has an influence, the greatest impact of
Christianity seems to be on what happens to property and
on what happens to women.

Christian influence is associated with substantially greater
conflict over property, with substantially less property destruction, and with the presence of inheritance rules for real
(as opposed to movable) property. These findings suggest
that Christianity comes with the accumulation of property
or with attitudes toward property that move people away
from nonownership of property or from communal ownership of property in the direction of individual ownership.
It may be surprising to some readers to learn that greater
conflict over property is associated with Christianity and

at the same time that the presence of inheritance rules for real property is also associated with Christianity. Some people might feel that inheritance rules should reduce conflict, so that anything positively associated with rules should be negatively associated with conflict. However, inheritance rules are usually more like guidelines than like absolute prescriptions, and even where they are strong prescriptions, there is always the possibility of dispute. Several individuals may feel that they have valid claims, there may be disagreement over what actually is inheritable or over what precise arrangement fits the rules. An irony in the relation of Christianity to the property variables is that it seems to indicate that Christianity, which might be thought by some to be of service to the spirit, actually seems to bring with it —or at least not to dispel at all effectively—a substantial concern with things material. The proposition "where Christianity, there materialism" seems to fit our data.

Christianity seems to have an effect on women. Degree of Christian influence is associated with less polygyny to a marginal extent and with later age of marriage for females. Christianity seems, in the case of marriage, to move women toward what may be a more powerful position. Where there is Christianity, a woman will be less likely to have to compete with cowives or be subordinate to a senior cowife; and where there is Christianity, it is less likely that a young girl will marry a mature man and thereby have her comparative immaturity as a possible source of subservience (cf. Cohen 1967: 39-40). Our suspicion is that the principal dynamic is that Christianity reduces polygyny, and that once polygyny is reduced, there is less pressure for early marriage of women. Early age of marriage for women seems to us to be most likely to occur where there is a shortage of more mature women due to polygyny.

For widows, Christianity is associated with a longer duration of mourning and a marginally smaller percentage of levirate remarriages. Some of the effect may be due to the ending of polygyny. Once polygyny is ended, there will be less demand for women. Fewer mature men will be single, and married men will not see widows or other single women as the means of increasing their own status or wealth. Hence, if the advent of Christianity means the ending of polygyny, it could easily make for a longer duration of widow mourning and less pressure to remarry by the levirate simply because of the reduction in demand for single women.

Christianity is also associated with less isolation for widows and less cleansing of females as part of death ceremonies. We wonder whether the isolation and cleansing effects are not dynamically connected with the age of marriage. Women marrying at an early age may be more strongly tied to their husbands. When a husband dies, they may experience a more intense loss due to the greater attachment developed through contact and dependence begun at an early age. Consequently their anger may be greater at the husband's death (hence the need for greater isolation), and their need to have the ties with him cut through ceremonial activity may be greater, hence the need for ceremonial cleansing of females.

Although one might casually assume that Christianity would have a most profound effect on the death customs and ideology of a society, our data suggest to the contrary that the impact of Christianity lies principally in its impact on property and on women. In the end, these influence death customs, but were Christianity to tolerate plural marriage and to be associated with less emphasis on the material, it might have almost no impact on the death customs and beliefs of the peoples who adopt it. It seems, in light of the data we have and our speculation about the meaning of these data, that the prevalence of Christianity in America is not a factor of overwhelming importance in understanding grief and mourning in America or in considering possible changes in American mourning customs in the areas considered in Chapters 2-5. The one notable factor to consider is that Christianity is associated with a lower level of property destruction.

Chapter 7

Grief and Mourning in America

Emotional Catharsis, Drugs, and Return to Outside Activities

Detailed, probing studies involving direct observation of grief processes of typical bereaved Americans are scarce. If one can generalize from personal experiences, literature, films, scholarly writings based on clinical cases, and retrospective accounts by persons who were bereaved, it would seem that bereaved Americans typically experience grief intensely and have considerable difficulty adjusting to the changed situation. Several recommendations for dealing with adjustment problems are common in the scholarly and popular literature dealing with grief.

A recommendation we discussed in Chapter 2 is that the catharsis of grief be encouraged in bereaved Americans. The assumption underlying this recommendation is that Americans often suppress emotional reactions in a way that disrupts their lives and that prevents or delays their return to a normal life without the person who has died. There is a clinical literature which shows that some people do get into serious difficulty as a result of unvented emotion (e.g. Bach and Wyden 1968). But what of the typical bereaved person?

The typical bereaved person may not be in need of help in catharsis of grief. Pressures to express more emotion may force the person to express feelings that are not felt or that are expressed in other ways or in other situations. It seems clear from the data presented in Chapter 1 that many bereaved persons in other cultures get along with little or no public crying and little or no public expression of anger or aggression. This may mean that it is common for bereaved persons to experience emotion not in need of catharsis or to vent emotion briefly, privately, or in ways that are relatively unspectacular. There may well be some Americans who can work through grief internally, or privately, or subtly without any psychological cost.

The writings of Freud have been a major impetus for recommendations of the catharsis of held-in feelings. His writings have provided the foundations of the psychological healing professions and have pervaded the culture. Originally the notion of psychological catharsis was one of venting strong emotions in the presence of a clinical practitioner. It is appropriate for a person trained to deal with catharsis of strong emotion to encourage, support, and channel it; but it may be risky for untrained individuals, who themselves may have defenses that would interact with cathartic emotion in an explosive or damaging way, to urge catharsis. Thus, even if catharsis might be of value, it may be a serious mistake to encourage it in the absence of a specialist with competence to deal with it. It seems undesirable to tell the layperson, as does a leaflet distributed by the American Funeral Directors Association ("Should I Go to the Funeral? What Do I Say?"), that: "Studies of mourning show that it is therapeutic to talk about the deceased. . . . [I]t is good to encourage an outward expression of feeling. . . . Encourage the mourner to tell you what he feels. . . ." These recommendations may be worthwhile for many, but may create difficulties in some cases. Emotion vented at people not trained to cope with it may risk a rupture of relationships, severe embarrassment, and guilt feelings for the bereaved or the person encouraging the catharsis. It could conceivably lead a bereaved person to doubt personal sanity, to adopt inappropriate mourning practices, or to feel weak, incompetent, or irreligious.

Another frequent recommendation for dealing with grief is that bereaved people be given drugs—usually sedatives, antidepressives, or tranquilizers. Of course, some bereaved persons may have a need for pharmacological therapy, but many who receive drugs may not need them. In some cases, drugs may be prescribed because the bereaved person is behaving in a way that seems inappropriate by somebody else's standards or that is threatening to somebody else. For example a recently bereaved widow may be inclined to direct angry accusations at the physician who cared for her deceased husband (cf. Glick, Weiss, and Parkes 1974: 57; Marris 1958: 18), to stay awake most of the night with a torrent of free associations streaming through her mind, or to cry and say strong words for many hours each day. A relative, clergyman, physician, or friend may feel that her behavior is inappropriate or be uncomfortable with it and may, as a consequence, urge drugs on the woman (cf. Maddison and Raphael 1972; Silverman 1972; Wiener 1972). Yet the problem may not be that of the bereaved person but of the person who, with different values about proper bereavement behavior or with discomfort in the face of the bereavement behavior, urges that drugs be given. What the widow is doing may be quite healthy working through of grief. Yet with the help of drugs taken at the urging of well-meaning people at a time when she may be quite influenceable, the widow's working-through process may be arrested (cf. Kubler-Ross 1972; Maddison and Raphael 1972; Parkes 1972: chap. 10).

Another possibility is that a bereaved person may ask for medical assistance or for drugs when what is really sought is satisfaction of the great dependency needs of bereavement. There are few situations in which American adults have as much practice and feel as much legitimate right to be dependent as in interaction with a physician. It may be that the seeking of medical assistance in bereavement represents, in some cases, a need for guidance and help which comes out as it does only because the seeking of medicine to deal with physical ills is an easy, known path to assistance. Then the physician prescribing sleeping pills or tranquilizers may, though giving what is requested and in part satisfying dependence needs, miss the point of the request (cf. Maddison and Raphael 1972). In such cases, physicians may be much more helpful if they refer bereaved persons to organizations, agencies, and clinicians with special competence to help bereaved people.

Another issue over which recommendations are common for bereaved persons concerns the resumption of normal, outside-the-home activity, such as going to work, attending school, and participating in organizations. In some cases, bereaved persons delay returning to work, school, or other outside activities quite a long time after a death and are criticized for doing this. In other cases, bereaved persons return quickly to such activities and are criticized for doing this or are encouraged to blame the activities for any bereavement difficulties experienced. There is probably quite a bit of variability in the degree to which outside-the-home activities will be disrupted by grief or disrupt working-through processes. Consequently, strong prescriptions about when to return to such activities seem impossible.

It may be that prompt return to outside activities by bereaved persons, whether it is a good thing or not, results from a lack of institutionalized practices for bereavement (e.g. a standard mourning period or a standard, ample bereavement furlough for employed people). Without clear guidelines to follow and without institutional supports, bereaved people may be inclined to minimize difficulties by minimizing the changes in their patterns of living. Bereaved persons may choose to behave as much as possible as they did before the death occurred, in order to avoid making decisions, to avoid having more blocks of time with no well-laid-out things to do, to avoid friction with others, and to avoid inconveniencing others. But by so behaving they may in some cases create difficulties for themselves and for the people around them. The difficulties for themselves include the cost of controlling feelings, the problem of having temporarily to avoid dealing with compelling concerns (e.g. confusion about the future or believing that one has interacted with a ghost). The difficulties in relationships include giving others conflicting messages about whether to be condolent or not— acting as though condolences are unnecessary and then resenting their absence (cf. Gorer 1965: 62)—and giving people who have not directly experienced bereavement the possibly erroneous impression that bereavement will not be very trying for them.

Death Ceremonies in America

Final Ceremonies

Americans seem in need of much more elaboration of death ceremony (Gorer 1965, 1973; Mandelbaum 1959; Volkart and Michael 1957). They would benefit, as we argued in Chapter 5, from time-limiting of bereavement, such as that which results from final funeral ceremonies. They might benefit from increased ritualization of death ceremonies in general, from practices that take into account realistically the disorganization, anger, fear, dependency, and other needs and emotions common to bereaved persons. One could argue, however, that there is more ritualization in America than appears at first glance. The body disposal alternatives, despite the choice points, are relatively well defined and get bereaved persons through the first few days of bereavement. Coping with the Social Security bureaucracy, insurance companies, wills and probate processes, and laws dealing with bank accounts and other assets also constitutes a kind of ritual and provides a sense of something to do. Memorial Day services and repeated opportunities for attendance at funerals and memorial services for friends and relatives of one's own and of one's acquaintances may also constitute institutionalized mechanisms for moving one through one's grief (cf. Warner 1961: chaps. 5 and 6). There are, however, undeveloped possibilities for time-limiting bereavement and underexploited opportunities for helping people through the bereavement process.

One possibility, which we have already discussed in some detail in Chapter 5, is to institute some kind of final funeral ceremony. It could be most conveniently linked to the first anniversary of a death, to a stone dedication, to Memorial Day, or to some other significant calendrical event, provided sufficient time has passed. Obviously, the institutionalization of a final ceremony would have to be harmonious with the practices of organized religions. Institutionalization would hinge on the widespread adoption of the practice, support from religious groups, widespread publicity, and explanations that fit the diverse belief systems that are to be found in America.

A serious attempt to institutionalize final funeral ceremonies would have to be strong enough to neutralize the sources of motivation for prolonging mourning. People might prolong mourning out of respect for the deceased, out of fear of the choice points that they would have to face once they ended mourning—because the mourning provided an excuse for something they wanted to continue to do (e.g. isolate themselves from others, get sympathy from others, not work)—and, of course, because they had failed to work through their grief. Working through may be delayed because one does not want to deal with feelings of guilt or anger, because one does not want to take responsiblility for disposing of reminders of the deceased, because one fears exploring new relationships, and for a large variety of other reasons. Institutionalization would provide strong support from relatives, friends, and others who have contact with a bereaved person. The widespread commemoration in America of birthdays and wedding anniversaries, the widespread distribution of gifts at Christmas, and the special attention given New Year's Day all are signs that Americans of diverse backgrounds can be united in institutionalized activities. Thus institutionalized final funeral ceremonies seem both desirable and feasible.

An alternative or supplement to institutionalized final ceremonies would be to develop organizations for bereaved persons. There are, for example, widow-to-widow programs (Hiltz 1975; Silverman 1972) designed to mobilize the wisdom and experience of widows of long standing to help recent widows. There are organizations such as Parents Without Partners for widowed persons with children. There are, here and there, other visible organizations for bereaved persons (see Parkes 1972: chap. 10 for a brief discussion and listing). Many churches and family service organizations provide opportunities for bereaved or unmarried persons or for single parents to get together. One may have reservations about the possibility of people without adequate training in counseling trying to help others. It is too easy to persuade others that their problems are like one's own when they are not, or to push people into "coping" strategies that are anything but coping for them. Nonetheless, any social institution that moves a bereaved person into and along a working-through process may be of value to many bereaved persons. One obvious problem in operating such institutions is that of matching up people who need it with the help available. People most in need might be least likely to join a voluntary organization. Organizational publicity may help, but there are likely to be bereaved persons who would not be inclined to join a voluntary organization for bereaved persons. Perhaps the element of voluntariness could be reduced or the incentives for attendance increased if participating in organizations of bereaved persons were a requirement of receipt of death benefits from insurance companies, unions, and penison plans, or if membership in such organizations were an available or automatic benefit from the various sources of death benefits.

A third possibility is better publicity for the services now available through family service agencies, community mental health programs, clergy who counsel, psychiatrists, and so on. Many people are unaware of the help that is available. Of those who are, some think that using such help is a sign of moral insufficiency, poverty, mental illness, or undesirable dependency. A campaign to make services for people with problems more visible and less stigmatized might help (cf. Rosenblatt and Phillips 1975).

Parallels in other societies exist, particularly in the case of the voluntary organizations and the mental health services. There may be an organizing of bereaved persons, particularly widows, and there may be healing rites available to distressed bereaved persons. However, optional participation may be absent in the case of organizations for bereaved persons in other societies, and stigmatization may not be a problem in the case of using healers.

Still another means of promoting working through in America might be simply giving publicity and acceptance to the enormous range of ways of expressing grief. If given permission, in effect, to cry or not to cry, to experience ghost cognitions, to be angry with others, to be interested in re-marrying or not, and so on, bereaved persons might not so often find themselves in problem situations.

Funerals

As we indicated in Chapter 2, there is considerable criticism of American funeral practices and a movement to provide bereaved persons with alternatives to dealing with a funeral director. (See Fulton 1961, Mitford 1963, and Vernon 1970: chap. 9 for summaries of criticisms of American funeral practices.) It seems that as long as funeral directors profit from deaths, some people are going to feel bitter. This bitterness can have many sources. Some may feel that it is wrong to profit from the losses of others, and some will suspect that funeral director profits are large and/or variable and conclude that at least some funeral directors are exploiting the bereaved. Another source of bitterness is the anger of normal bereavement, an anger that is available to direct at any-one with whom the bereaved comes in contact. There is also the anger that develops for some bereaved persons when a funeral director insists that choices be made. The anger will stem from having to make choices when one does not feel like making them and from having made salient (1) guilt feelings and (2) the conflict that Americans often feel between treating a corpse as an inanimate and decomposing residue and treating it as an object of great significance.

The bitterness and anger directed at funeral directors might be reduced by preselected funeral plans (e.g. the memorial society), which circumvent some conflicts and the pain of making choices by having choices made beforehand. However, it may be that often the preselection is so open-ended that the bereaved still feel that they are at choice points when the funeral arrangements are made. Another way of reducing bitterness and anger might be to eliminate choices at funerals. Instead of the usual array of alternatives, there might be a single standard coffin, funeral cortege, treatment of the body, and so on. However, many Americans seem inclined to prefer choices or to spend more than a minimal amount of money whenever an important ceremony occurs. A third way of mitigating bitterness and anger might be to control or eliminate profit from funeral practices. This could be done through having fixed costs, fixed profits, or having funerals carried out as public, tax-supported services. There would, in any case, still be the problem of dealing with the normal anger and aggression of bereavement. Although ritual specialists might help with the control of this anger and aggression, there still would be a capacity to develop anger, indignation, or the like at those who manage and carry out funerals.

Reducing Choice Alternatives

More generally, bereaved persons in America are faced with many choices in the first few days following a death. These choices augment whatever frustration, anger, and disorganization there might already be as a result of the death. One must choose to have a eulogy said or not (and if so, there may be no standard guidelines to eulogy content and format); one must choose to have an open coffin or not; one must choose the degree of publicity of ceremonies and perhaps the location of ceremonies and the officiants; one must decide what to do about hospitality for bereaved persons from out of town and for those paying condolence calls, and so on. For acquaintances of the bereaved, there is no well-publicized, widely accepted procedure for visiting and no well-publicized, widely accepted message to deliver. This lack of norms for expressing condolences creates difficulties and increases the chances of the acquaintances saying or doing something (or failing to say or do something) that offends the bereaved person. A cost of choice and diversity, then, lies in the friction that can occur at each choice point. Gorer (1973), noting that many Americans lack religious involvement, has proposed that secular mourning rituals be adopted, partially analogous to secular wedding rituals. These might include both funeral practices and an etiquette for first contacts of people with their newly bereaved acquaintances. A widely accepted patterning of behavior for bereaved persons and for those dealing with them might well reduce the problems that, in America, surround a death. "At first sight, it seems false to impose custom on so internal and private an emotion as grief; yet the very loneliness of the crisis, and the intensity of ambivalence, cries out for a supportive structure" (Marris 1974: 86).

Education for Grief and Mourning

A high level of ritualization of death activities, coupled with a high death rate, provide strong education for grief and mourning in many societies. One cost of the "deritualization" (Gorer 1973; Mandelbaum 1959) of funeral activities in America and of American longevity is that American adults are less likely to know what to do when bereaved. There may be functional substitutes for direct experience; the national broadcast of a President's funeral, for example, will give many Americans an opportunity to learn about some aspects of grief and mourning. An increase in ritualization of grief and mourning activities might also help to educate people and thereby reduce uncertainty about proper bereavement behavior.

Uncertainty about proper behavior, as we have suggested earlier in this book, may lead many to do their grieving in private. They fear censure for behaving inappropriately, or they wish to avoid the costs of having to behave in a way they think others think they should behave. They may fear the risk to relationships of relaxing control on anger and aggression, and of course they may fear burdening others with their emotions and needs. However understandable, the conditions that promote privacy increase problems for all by making it harder for others to know what is proper, acceptable, normal, and tolerable grief behavior. Effectively providing permission for a much broader range of public grief behaviors might in the long run lead to education for grief and mourning through greater opportunity to observe the grief and mourning of others. This education might then reduce the stress of bereavement for many.

Some social critics have argued that in America there is considerable denial of death. By this they mean that Americans tend to behave as if people do not die, as if somebody who has died has not died, or as if they themselves will not die. The implication of these critics is that some kind of repression, some failure to see compelling reality, is a part of the culture. This may be so, but it also may be that what seems like denial is actually realistic behavior in the face of the facts of death in America. The facts are (1) that most people live quite a long time, so that many will be quite old before they experience the death of someone close to them, (2) that the lack of elaborate death rituals reduces people's contact with death, and (3) that death in America is quite commonly out of sight of most, because of the American use of hospitalization to prolong life and minimize pain. Moreover, what seems like denial in early bereavement may merely be the residue of the response dispositions we discussed at length in Chapters 3 and 4. People may not be denying reality; they may merely be suffering the normal lag that comes when old dispositions have to be replaced by new ones. They may be no more denying in a repressive sense than they would be if they were learning how to drive on the left after having driven for a long time on the right side of the road or learning how to navigate through the house after the furniture had been rearranged. Some people who are bereaved may engage in repressive mental activities, but the case for denial of death in America may have been too strongly stated. A look at American newspapers, films, and television, at the American concern with life insurance and the making of wills, and at the American concern for safety in the cities and on the highways suggests that Americans do face up to death quite a bit. Perhaps the issue is only one of how to define denial (Donaldson 1972; Vernon 1970: 31), but perhaps, too, there are empirical questions dealing with what Americans actually think about in the area of death (cf. Dumont and Foss 1972).

Although Americans may lack some kinds of death educative experiences—or be deficient in them—there is still a great deal of education for grief and mourning going on. Even small children have, for example, received intensive education in what to think about ghosts. Many Americans have been taught to think that it is a sign of maturity to control emotions. And in many a religious congregation, suggestions are made about the relation between religious faith and bereavement behavior. Thus, even if contemporary Americans have less education for grief and mourning than the aboriginal Iroquois or contemporary Egyptian Fellahin, for example, they still are educated to some extent.

Grief and Mourning for Losses Other than Deaths

Bowlby (1961) has been a leader among many who talk about grief and mourning behavior following losses other than a death. What if a parent leaves a child for a week or a day? What if a family moves to another community? What if a valued possession is lost? One could argue that people would experience symptoms of grief at such times and would benefit from following wise mourning practices. There is, of course, an opportunity to reduce the case to absurdity. Would anyone mourn a lost pencil or spilled milk? Perhaps one way to separate bereaving losses from losses for which discussions of grief would be absurd is to extend the analyses made in Chapters 3 and 4 of habitual patterns of behavior. Perhaps the greater the amount of patterned activity disrupted (as measured, perhaps, on a minutes per day basis) the more likely one is to experience grief and the greater the grief experienced. One advantage of such an analysis, in addition to circumventing absurdities, is that it avoids the question of love. There is a great deal said about loss of loved ones being bereaving, with the implication that strong bereavement is a sign of strong love. Yet many are the anecdotes of people expressing strong grief at death of a hated spouse or parent. Without independent measures of love, it seems unproductive and misleading to talk about love and bereavement (Lindemann 1944; Mandler 1964). Strong bereavement may be more realistically a sign of broken habitual patterns than of lost love. One can even argue that love is a substitute for other bonds and, as such, is likely to be strongest before habitual patterns bind one to a spouse or infant (Coppinger and Rosenblatt 1968; Rosenblatt 1974b). There may, however, be a relationship between love and habitual patterns, in that spouses who love each other strongly may have a larger fraction of daily habit linked to the presence and activities of the other. Even if that were so, it is by no means clear that love is a necessary prerequisite to the experience of very intense bereavement.

If it is correct to speak of grief and mourning in the case of losses other than those due to a death, then it may be productive to apply our theoretical analyses and findings to such losses. Consider separation and divorce in our society. One spouse generally leaves the previously shared residence; the other does not. Of course it is quite common for the fact of divorce to have been anteceded by a rending of relationships that has brought the couple far down the road toward maximum tie-breaking. But in cases in which separation or divorce is not preceded by relatively complete tie-breaking, the acquisition of new relationships should, according to the theory and findings discussed in Chapter 4, differ between a spouse who changes residence and one who does not. The one who remains in the residence will have many reminders of the spouse who has left, and these reminders will inhibit acquiring a new marital type of relationship. The one who leaves the residence will lack these inhibitions and should have an easier time of acquiring new relationships. If we are right, divorce property settlements may be looked at from a new perspective. It is not totally a victory to keep possession of one's house and furniture; rather, it is in some ways a burden. Of course a formal study of spouse differences in resumption of a marital type of relationship would have to control for differences in social ecology, since one person may be much more often in social situations conducive to acquiring new relationships. But it seems to us that in divorce, as in the case of death of a spouse, familiar environmental stimuli provide reminders of the old relationship that impede changes in dispositions and make acquisition of any new relationship more difficult.

Extending the analysis of possible grief in divorce, we might expect that rapid adjustment to divorce would be promoted by stimulus changes that reduce evocation of old response patterns. Thus, moving furniture, redecorating the dwelling, changing eating routines, changing styles of clothing all could promote adjustment to divorce.

Although abandoning one's residence and neighborhood may facilitate the acquisition of new patterns of behavior, as was suggested in Chapter 4, a change in residence might also create grief (Fried 1963). Grief for a lost residence was discussed in Chapter 4. A move that deprives one of the cues that are important to one's identity and way of life and that makes it more difficult to carry on one's friendships, one's avocational activities, and one's familiar shopping routines may be quite disruptive and bereaving. Among other things, this suggests that grief as a result of moving may be somewhat reduced if one moves only a short distance. In such a case, one can retain neighborhood friendships, familiar shopping patterns, and other familiar patterns linked to one's neighborhood.

In the case of changing residence, there might well be the analog of ghosts—illusions of being in the old residence and behaving as though still in the old residence (for example getting out of bed on the side that was appropriate in the old residence but not the new).

Retirement can also be expected to produce grief reactions. A person who retires can be expected to be bereaved as a result of the termination of so much habitual behavior, even if the job left was disliked. Grief resulting from retirement could be expected to lead to ghosts—illusions of still being on the job. Such grief could also be expected to be reduced if stimuli to the old work are not present. Thus, grief could be greater at retirement for a person who did some of the past work at home, who lives near to the place of work, and who retains tools, garments, and publications used in the work. Perhaps in the case of retirement, as in the case of death, there needs to be a final ceremony. Such a ceremony could commit a retiring person to a new pattern of living and commit the person's friends and relatives to be supportive of that new pattern of living. At many places of employment there are parties for people who are about to retire, but these, like initial funeral ceremonies, may not be adequate. If, in addition, there were some sort of ceremonial event six months or a year after the retirement, at which the retired person is incorporated into the society of retired persons and is expected to make a strong commitment to the day-to-day activities of retirement, retirement might be less difficult.

In the case of a child leaving home (e.g. to college, to marry, to the military), grief might be present both for the leaver and the left. As in the case of divorce, the problems might be greater for the left, who continue to be faced with the old relationship stimuli. The problem would be especially great for persons with a comparatively large number of patterns of behavior disrupted—e.g. parents who have no other child left at home, a sibling who shared a room with the leaver. In these cases, ghosts can easily be expected—illusions of the presence of the leaver—and tie-breaking, such as altering reminders, might be of help.

Vacations away from home might be a special case of grief-creating situations (Rosenblatt and Russell 1975). The vacation is supposed to help one to get away from daily work routines, but perhaps for all people grieving for the lost work (agitation, anger, feelings of frustration, feelings of not having enough to do) might be present. As a consequence, people who go on vacations may feel angry with one another and frustrated. It may help, however, to minimize reminders of the old routine—e.g. for the scholar to bring no scholarly work along and for the housewife to stay away from housework situations—and to routinize vacations so that there are clear-cut, well-learned patterns of activity to engage in.

Marris (1974) has analyzed loss and change in a variety of situations from the perspective of grief. He has chosen to focus on loss of purpose and of old understandings of reality as the key grief elements operating in various loss and change situations. We, in contrast, have chosen to emphasize changes in habitual patterns of behavior and the compellingness of familiar cues to engage in old patterns of behavior as key elements in the discussion of grief for losses other than a death. There is no doubt that an analysis in terms of purposes and understandings will lead one into different speculations and hypotheses than an analysis in terms of familiar stimuli and habitual patterns of behavior. Nonetheless, the perspective of Marris and the perspective we take overlap a great deal. We talk about no longer appropriate patterns of behavior and then go on to talk about stimuli influencing those patterns and the difficulty in changing those patterns. But the reason those patterns are no longer appropriate is that old purposes and understandings are no longer appropriate.

Marris discusses at great length the conflict one experiences in grief over any loss between retaining old purposes and understandings and acquiring new ones. He argues that the old cannot be simply forgotten without invalidating current activities and that the old purposes and understandings are not eliminated but somehow incorporated into a new version of purposes and understandings. Working through would, in his argument, involve a working through of the conflict. One could read our discussion of ties and tie-breaking, particularly in Chapter 4, as contradicting Marris's position, but we think there is no contradiction. From our point of view, until a person acknowledges that a loss has occurred, there is no possibility of resuming a normal life without the deceased. Once one has acknowledged the loss and begins to seek a new pattern of life, then the person must cope with considerable response conflict. Whether the old purposes and understandings are incorporated into the new patterns may be problematic. But to the extent that people seek to live in some ways as they did before a loss and to the extent that the relationship one had with the deceased before the death occurred has altered one, then we do not disagree with Marris.

Some Pressing Research Needs

For future cross-cultural studies of grief and mourning, the greatest need is for numerous detailed ethnographic accounts. Such accounts will enable more stringent tests of the hypotheses we have discussed in this monograph and will enable examination of a much wider range of hypotheses. There have been, since the time we began our research, a few elaborate ethnographic accounts of at least some aspects of death customs, most notably those by Ahern (1973) and by Bloch (1971). Recent works by Toynbee (1971) on ancient Rome and by Kurtz and Boardman (1971) on ancient Greece also seem useful.

In any area of ethnographic work, it is much easier to focus on a topic if there are theories indicating that some kinds of data are worth examining. There is, in any society, such a chaos of information that ethnographers must be highly selective. We hope that it is a contribution of this monograph to focus the attention of ethnographers on the areas for which we have provided some theory—emotional behavior, ghost beliefs and cognitions, tie-breaking customs, and final funeral ceremonies.

There were a number of topic areas we had to drop, because we could not find strong enough ethnographic information. We hope that anthropologists will, in the future, provide data in these areas. The areas include: variations in grief and mourning customs associated with various kinds of death (infant, elderly, female vs. male, high status vs. low status, accidental death vs. natural death); intracommunity conflict and resentment over succession to responsibility and ownership; premortem allocation of property and roles; attitudes of bereaved persons toward those who provided much or little help during the bereavement period; the questions of who gives how much of what kinds of help to bereaved persons, and of who handles a corpse, how, and for how long; taboos on work activities of the bereaved; sources of variation in persistence and behavior of spirits of the dead; sources of variations in means of body disposal; naming of babies after deceased persons; verbal expressions concerning recently deceased persons; and details of who attends what ceremonies.

There is also a vast array of death-related topics which could conceivably be studied cross-culturally but which we did not begin to study. These include: mourning terms; body preparation; symbolism in decoration of mourners; pollution rules relating to contact with the possessions of the deceased and the principal mourners; folktales about the dead and death; the influence on grief of the degree of interdependence with the person who dies; and the kinds of events that turn emotional expression on and off. One could also study such topics as: whether there are differences between cultures in demand for emotional expression or suppression, and (if there are), what other aspects of culture are related; the relationship cross-culturally between bereavement and health, eating, work, sleep, and other factors discussed in the literature on grief in Western culture; and the influence of the formal kinship system of a culture on who expresses what emotions.

We purposely avoided dealing with the last topic, although it could be of central interest to somebody who approached the area of grief from the perspective of social anthropology.

We suspect that in the area of death, anthropologists may be blinded to significant phenomena by the importance of customs dealing with structural problems. If a man dies, his wife may not play a prominent part in ceremony nor be the focus of many customs. Instead, members of his kin group may play key roles, be labeled principal mourners, and even provide the most dramatic public display of emotion. We do not want to belittle the impact of a person's death on the person's kin, but our documentation of the role of tie-breaking in remarriage suggests that, even where ceremonies focus on bereaved people other than the spouse, the history of attachment of the spouse is a factor of importance. Although it may appear that a spouse is not a principal mourner, the magnitude of the spouse's grief may be as great as anyone else's and customs dealing with the grief of that spouse may be well developed.

We were repeatedly frustrated in our research by the ambiguity of ethnographic accounts concerning the basis of the assertions that were made. We had difficulty in many cases knowing whether we were reading about norms or about behavior; about behavior actually observed by the ethnographer or only recounted by informants. Was it a summary of statements by many informants, by a few, or just one? Or was it just the ethnographer's best guess, based on inference? In many cases it is quite crucial that we separate norms from behavior. No doubt it is inconvenient for an ethnographer to indicate with each statement what its basis is. But the inconvenience is overbalanced by the great value of such detailed epistemic information. Perhaps we are asking for restrictions on writing style for ethnographers, that ethnographers say who said what, where what was observed, and in how many instances. It certainly is not an unusual demand to ask of scholars that they indicate their sources of information. We are not saying that it is illegitimate to report impressions, guesses, and statements with little or no backing in direct observation, but it would be exceedingly helpful if these were indicated as such.

There is also a need for something—research or differentiation of terms—in the area of denial (Dumont and Foss 1972). One problem seems to be that the term "denial" is applied all too often to the behavior of persons who seem unemotional in the face of a death or who give little indication that they are anticipating death for themselves or for someone else. There is quite a difference between a person not thinking at all about death and a person who thinks about it but expresses little. Actually, the mechanisms underlying what gets labeled as denial may be quite diverse.

Another area that seems worthy of future research is the area of commitment to accepting a death, an area which we discussed in Chapter 5. There is a substantial number of acts, from culture to culture, which seem to express publicly the acknowledgment if not the acceptance by a bereaved person that a death has occurred. In American culture, these acts include making decisions about the funeral process and disposal of the body, engaging in the legal activities following a death, public reviewal of the corpse, and throwing dirt into a grave (cf. Vernon 1970: 146). Writing a eulogy for a deceased friend or relative also seems to be an act of commitment. Careful study of commitment might illuminate issues relating to denial. It could also allow for a clearer understanding of the first, numbed stage of grief. Are committing acts engaged in during this period somehow less effective? Or are they quite effective? If they are effective, the apparent numbness may belie a great deal of cognitive and emotional work on the part of the bereaved person. Research in this area could provide a greater understanding of a broad range of funeral practices in the United States and in other cultures and lead to a greater understanding of the effects of all ceremonial acts.

Chapter Summary

In this chapter we have discussed a number of aspects of grief and mourning in America from the perspective of our theories and findings. We have dealt with the catharsis of grief, the administration of drugs to bereaved persons, the question of when a bereaved person should return to daily activities, the ritualization of American mourning practices and its alternatives, the questions that have been raised concerning funeral directors, the problem of choices in American death customs, denial of death, and education for grief and mourning. We have also discussed grief and mourning for losses other than a death—e.g. losses at a divorce, at a change in residence, at retirement, on vacation, and at the moving away of someone who has been coresident with one. Finally, we have reviewed some research needs, pointing to a small part of the vast amount of cross-cultural research that might be worthwhile to do and indicating some important areas for research within American culture.

Concluding Statement for the Book

In this comparative study of seventy-eight world cultures, an ethnocentric perspective has often been productive. Despite warnings (Volkart and Michael 1957) that American mourning customs and grief behavior may be peculiar to America, it seems that American practices and behaviors are a relatively safe base from which to generalize about the species. We have assumed in our research that people everywhere experience grief, that people everywhere experience the death of close kin as a loss and mourn for that loss. Judging by the richness of our findings, our assumptions have been correct. Apparently the nature of human interaction and long-term relations are such that, despite a wide range of differences among cultures, people around the world experience grief and commonly have the opportunity to express it.

This book has provided a demonstration of the value of ritual specialists and of marking and isolation in the control of anger and aggression in bereavement. Evidence has been presented concerning the residues of ties to a deceased person, the salience of ghost cognitions as one element of these residues, and the importance of tie-breaking customs in dealing with these residues. We have also provided documentation for the role of final funeral ceremonies in terminating grief, and we have examined the relationship of Christianity to the aspects of grief and mourning that we have studied.

Appendixes

Appendix.
Technical Details

0.0 Introduction: Methods

Good overviews of procedures and epistemological issues in cross-cultural research can be found in a book edited by Naroll and Cohen (1970) and in a chapter written by Whiting (1968).

0.1 Sampling

In sampling, our goal was a representative sample of 75 societies from around the world. Seventy-five seemed a reasonable compromise between the ideal of great statistical power and the reality of limited resources (limited time, finances, library facilities, and ethnographic literature dealing with grief and mourning). The sample we eventually arrived at consisted of 78 societies drawn from the universe of culture areas defined by Murdock and White in their "Standard Cross-Cultural Sample" (1969). Murdock and White developed a standard sample of 186 well-described societies, each from a different culture area, to provide a representative sample of cultures. We had to shop among their 186 societies, with the order of shopping determined by use of a random number table, to find ones that seemed to meet our two usability criteria. One of the usability criteria was that the death customs of a society appear to us to be adequately described, preferably with data on body disposal, attendance at ceremonies or reports that ceremonies were absent, behavior of bereaved persons, duration of mourning, fate of widows, presence or absence of ghost fear or fear of the dead, and disposal of property of deceased adults. The other criterion was that a society or one very similar to it must not have been a source of ideas in the research proposal that was submitted by Rosenblatt to the National Institute of Mental Health and which developed many of our hypotheses. Ten of the 78 societies in our sample are substitutes from the same culture areas as societies in the Murdock and White sample (Chippewa, Katab, Murngin, Seniang, Siwans, Tswana, Vanua Levu Fijians, Walbiri, Western Apache, and Zapotec). To determine what culture area a society was in, we consulted two catalogs of culture areas: Murdock's (1968) "World Sampling Provinces" and the "Ethnographic Atlas," which has been published cumulatively since 1962 in many issues of the quarterly journal called *Ethnology*. (A substantial portion of the Ethnographic Atlas has also been published separately—see Murdock 1967). When it became clear that a case in the Standard Cross-Cultural Sample was inadequate, we went to Murdock's World Sampling Provinces. If there were other societies listed in the province in which an inadequately described society was located, we examined the material that was available on them, taking them in the order listed by Murdock. In achieving the sample of 78 adequately described societies we had to look for or at materials from 120 societies. Many of the ones we did not use may be adequately described, but we were unable to find adequate materials through locally available resources. For every society, we tried to focus on a particular time period and a particular community or type of community.

The Ethnographic Atlas provided the bibliographic base of the Murdock and White sample. The Atlas also provides, for about 1,300 cultures, ratings of many cultural traits. We attempted to work with the ethnographic bibliography that was the basis of the Ethnographic Atlas ratings, so that we could use the Atlas ratings where those ratings might help us to understand our data better. However, in some cases we used sources different from or additional to those listed by Murdock and White.

For societies in the sample, we generally made our own extracts of published materials relevant to grief and mourning and the correlates of interest. But some sources could only be obtained from the Human Relations Area Files (HRAF), a compilation of ethnographic materials describing several hundred cultures, with material for each society grouped into each of a large number of categories—e.g. funerals, mourning. For sources that could only be obtained from HRAF, we relied on the extracts provided by the Files. We did our own translating of sources dealing with the Kafa and of sources dealing with several cases that we eventually decided, because of inadequate information, not to include in the sample of 78 societies.

Some of the societies in the sample no longer exist; other societies in the sample are by now quite a bit different from the way they were at the time of description. The disappearance or alteration of cultures in the sample does not, in our thinking, make our findings any less valid. Our interest is in characterizing the human species and the societies of that species. As long as the human species is represented in each case, it does not matter whether the society still exists or whether it is just as it was when it was described. Each society represents an instance of human responses to death and seems to us to be as valid a representation of the species as would be a description of a contemporary society. It may be true that a society could end because of grossly maladaptive death customs, but it is much more likely that recent and contemporary societies would end or change markedly through conquest and assimilation, through the ravages of disease, or through some form of modernization.

0.2 Rating Procedures

Some of the ratings of cultures that are discussed in this book were obtained from the Ethnographic Atlas, but most of the ratings we report were made by us and our raters. All the variables that were measured by us were rated by at least two raters, working independently of one another. Different variables were rated by different rater pairs or groups. The raters on this project were Teri-Christine Hall, Merrie Norman Harrison, Douglas A. Jackson, Paul C. Rosenblatt, Elizabeth Skoogberg, Elizabeth A. Syme, R. Patricia Walsh, and Richard Walz. Further on in this Appendix we list each

variable discussed in the book, its interrater reliability, and
the persons who made the ratings of it. Hall, Harrison, Skoogberg, Syme, and Walz were completely ignorant of the hypotheses that inspired our work. We were, nonetheless, concerned
about the possibility of unconscious bias by Rosenblatt, Walsh,
and Jackson in making ratings, biases that might distort
ratings to fit hypotheses. However, we feel confident that our
biases were not expressed in ratings, in part because of our
practice of using at least one person who was ignorant of the
hypotheses in each group of independent raters. For no
variables except the presence of final funeral ceremonies and
the degree of Christian influence was more than one of the
raters a coauthor of this book. The possibility of bias was
further reduced, because the raters were rarely in a position
to monitor or know hypothesized correlates of a variable
being rated. Moreover, bias was also minimized by the precision of the instructions, which left relatively little room
for subjective bias to operate.

Variables were included in intervariable analyses if they
could be measured with adequate convergent and discriminant validity (Campbell and Fiske 1959) and were measurable
in more than a few societies. Convergent validity in this
study is the extent to which different people making ratings
of the same variable independently arrived at the same
ratings for each society that both attempted to rate. For
discriminant validity, it was necessary that ratings by individual raters (and scores pooling separate sets of ratings of some
attribute) not be too strongly correlated with measures that
they should not be correlated with. These potential contaminating factors included the order in which raters rated the
societies and the sex of the ethnographer or ethnographers
who described each society. In deciding whether the ratings
of a variable by individual raters were good enough to combine, we required that each rater's ratings of a variable
generally correlate best with the other rater's ratings of the
same variable. Many ratings made on grief and mourning
for deceased infants, children, and elderly were dropped, for
example, because the ratings were more strongly correlated
across types of deceased person for a specific rater than across
raters for a specific grief or mourning measure.

The combined ratings of variables reported in this book represent simple adding or averaging of ratings with adequate validity. For variables rated on presence-absence by two raters, cases of disagreement were generally deleted. In combining ratings of presence-absence by four raters, a case was used only if three or four of the four raters agreed.

For most of the variables discussed in this book there is a substantial case loss from the original 78 societies. This is largely due to the combination of two factors that are difficult to separate, the limitations of the ethnographic literature in dealing with death-related topics and our ambitious attempts to study behaviors and culture traits that are rarely well described. Case loss makes generalization to the species problematic, but we doubt that we have systematically lost cases discrepant from or consistent with our hypotheses.

0.3 Diffusion Analysis

We tested the possibility that the culture traits that we hypothesized to be related might diffuse jointly. The term diffusion refers to the spread of culture traits from one culture to another with which it has some contact. Many scholars who read cross-cultural research have been concerned with the possibility that an apparently meaningful association between two variables might be due to random cultural diffusion (e.g. Driver and Chaney 1970; Naroll 1961). This is called Galton's problem, so called because it was first suggested by Sir Francis Galton in a public comment following a speech by E. B. Tylor (1889) on the comparative method. Scholars who worry about Galton's problem point out that statistical analyses assume independence of cases and that cultural diffusion between societies in a sample will produce nonindependence. Hence, these scholars believe that for data contaminated by cultural diffusion there is no meaning to statistical tests. We do not agree with this point of view, but we have done diffusion tests anyway. The one test that showed some indication of possible diffusion artifacts is reported in section 2.0 in this Appendix. In general, our diffusion test procedure involved the tracing of patterns of joint clustering of scores on pairs of variables being correlated

(Method Four of Naroll and D'Andrade 1963). Our sample was laid out on two diffusion paths, one north from Africa into Europe and one north through Oceania into Asia and then south through the Americas. In examining possible diffusion patterns, we used what might be called a conservative procedure, trying to maximize the apparent diffusion artifact through manipulating the order of societies on the diffusion path wherever such a manipulation seemed at all justifiable by the facts of geographical distances or temporal separation (some cultures were described hundreds of years before others). But doing this still yielded almost no suggestion of diffusion artifacts. Perhaps the weakness of joint cultural diffusion as an explanation for the obtained correlations should be no surprise. Our sample was small, and generally we had many missing cases in our correlational analyses as a result of inadequate data; this means that the cases involved in any analysis will generally be quite far apart, which reduces the chance that cultural diffusion will have occurred commonly among the cases. The working diffusion alignments used in our study are contained in the following two lists, along with the number of each society in our data records and our understanding of the focal longitude and latitude of each society.

North through Africa

64	32E 24S Thonga	46	11W 8N Mende
69	27E 24S Tswana	61	32E 10N Shilluk
44	16E 12S Mbundu	35	8E 10N Katab
43	36E 2S Masai	23	9E 12N Hausa
18	32E 1N Ganda	16	33E 25N Egyptian Fellahin
45	28E 2N Mbuti	63	26E 29N Siwans
05	27E 5N Azande	20	20E 42N Gheg
27	7E 6N Ibo	08	2W 43N Basque
32	36E 7N Kafa	38	22E 68N Lapps

*North through Oceania to Asia
and into the Americas*

74 132E 22S Walbiri	02 144E 44N Ainu
49 136E 12S Murngin	13 110W 69N Copper Eskimo
72 179E 17S Vanua Levu Fijians	17 145W 61N Eyak
59 167E 17S Seniang	34 128W 59N Kaska
56 170W 14S Samoans	11 96W 49N Chippewa
65 168E 12S Tikopia	21 109W 49N Gros Ventre
53 148E 9S Orokaiva	71 123W 48N Twana
67 151E 8S Trobrianders	24 101W 47N Hidatsa
06 115E 8S Balinese	47 65W 47N Micmac
30 110E 7S Javanese	26 78W 44N Huron
33 136E 4S Kapauku	36 122W 43N Klamath
41 147E 2S Manus	55 100W 42N Pawnee
58 101E 6N Semang	52 96W 41N Omaha
68 152E 7N Trukese	77 124W 41N Yurok
42 171E 7N Marshallese	76 120W 36N Wukchumni
73 81E 8N Vedda	75 110W 34N Western Apache
50 92E 9N Nicobarese	12 100W 33N Comanche
03 93E 12N Andamanese	54 112W 31N Papago
66 77E 12N Toda	22 72W 18N Haitians
07 100E 15N Thai villagers	78 96W 17N Zapotec
28 121E 17N Ifugao	48 85W 13N Miskito
25 80E 21N Hill Maria Gond	09 59W 5N Carib
51 96E 22N Burmese villagers	14 71W 1N Cubeo
57 87E 24N Santal	31 78W 4S Jivaro
19 91E 26N Garo	15 45W 7S Eastern Timbira
39 89E 28N Lepcha	70 35W 8S Tupinamba
40 103E 29N Lolo	60 52W 14S Shavante
10 120E 31N Chinese villagers	62 64W 16S Siriono
29 136E 35N Japanese	04 50W 28S Aweikoma
37 102E 35N Koreans	01 61W 29S Abipone

Critics concerned with cross-cultural methodology have pointed out that it is sometimes difficult to know where one society leaves off and another begins. They might argue, for example, that if there has been diffusion between Comanche and Chippewa it is difficult to decide whether they are two cultures or only one. In our study, the problem of cultural boundaries has in a sense been dealt with by use of published delineations of culture areas, those in the Ethnographic Atlas and in the papers by Murdock (1968) and by Murdock and White (1969). The concern of scholars worried about cultural boundaries is also taken into account by the diffusion tests we have done. If there were many cultural boundary problems in the data, it would appear that joint diffusion of culture traits correlated was common.

0.4 Data Quality Control

Naroll (1962) has alerted cross-cultural researchers to the possibility of data contamination and has suggested a variety of ingenious means for detecting such contamination. We have tried to prevent several artifacts from contaminating our data. We have correlated ratings with the order in which they were made. This provides protection from rater fatigue or other changes in the rater over the course of rating. We have added sex of ethnographers as a quality control variable, primarily to protect us against contaminated sex difference data. And we have used the proportion of our first 118 variables in which a society could be rated as an indicator of information adequacy. We used this indicator as a basis for weeding out variables for which scores seemed to be an artifact of information adequacy. It would be a mistake, for example, to use a variable scored "present" or "absent" if all the cases with a rating of "present" were cases with high information adequacy and all the cases with a rating of "absent" were cases with low information adequacy. In such a situation, one might suspect that all cases actually had the culture trait present, but that all those with relatively inadequate information simply lacked reports of the information necessary to make the rating of "present."

0.5 On Statistics

The results of the statistical analyses underlying our assertions are tabulated in this Appendix. We have endeavored to write a book that could be read by people with no training in statistics, yet statistical analysis has been important in our epistemology. To simplify matters for the reader, we have used the Pearson product-moment correlation in almost every case where we have done a statistical analysis. The product-moment correlation has the following properties. It ranges from +1.00 through .00 to -1.00. If the correlation is positive, that means that as values on one variable increase, values on the other variable also increase. If the correlation is negative, that means that as values on one variable increase, values on the other variable decrease. Generally the correlation coefficient is an index of the strength of the relationship or the amount of association between one variable and the other.

In our data, the correlation coefficient is an indicator of monotonic relationship, not of linear relationship. It would be an indicator of linear relationship only if our scales of measurement were known to be equal interval. We do not know that to be the case, so the difference between, say, 02 and 04 on a scale of importance of ritual specialists up to and including initial disposal of a body may be quite different from the difference between 08 and 10 on that scale. Therefore, we are in a position to talk only about monotonic relationships.

Another desirable property of the correlation coefficient is that its square is equal to the proportion of variance on one variable that can be predicted from the other. Thus we can tell how much variance is accounted for by the monotonic trend of a relationship and also how much is left unaccounted for. Such a consideration provides an estimation of the practical significance of a relationship and of the extent to which there is more to be learned about factors controlling, controlled by, or related to the dimensions of interest.

The product-moment correlation has some failings. We are alerted to these and have tried to take them into account. One of them is that a single unusual case may alter a coefficient

markedly. If, for example, all the cases but one in some analysis
have the same scores on the two dimensions being correlated,
and if the other case has a different score on both dimensions,
a correlation of 1.00 or -1.00 will result. It would be risky to
base strong practical recommendations on the uniqueness
of that single case. The single case may have been erroneously
measured, or it may be like no other case in the universe. To
guard against such a possibility, we have looked at contingency
tables and done other statistics on every significant correlation
discussed in this book. Where the correlation coefficient seems
misleading or untrustworthy because of one or two unique
cases, we have so indicated in this Appendix.

Another failing of the correlation coefficient is that it cannot
get close to 1.00 or -1.00 if the dimensions being correlated
have distributions with markedly different shapes. For
example if two dichotomously scored measures are being
correlated and the 30 cases for which we have data on both
measures are distributed 15-15 on one measure and 4-26 on the
other, the greatest obtainable correlation is .39, which falls
far short of 1.00 or -1.00. We have decided to take the correlation coefficient in such cases on face and, in some analyses,
to consider hypotheses to be falsified on the basis of correlations
that are as strong as they can be but fall short of statistical
significance. The reason for this is that the correlation coefficient remains, even in these cases, a good indicator of the
degree to which a score of a case on one variable can be predicted through knowing its score on another variable.

In defense of the correlation coefficient, we can point out
that other statistics may be less powerful given our small
numbers of cases, may require arbitrary cutoffs to be made
in order to set up the necessary categories for statistical
computation, and may require arbitrary decisions about what
to do about cases that have identical scores on one or both
measures being correlated. The correlation coefficient is an
adequate, all-purpose statistic. It can be used with all variables in this study. Its use facilitates reading and understanding
for people with little background in statistics. Its use throughout the study makes it easy to compare strengths of relationships in different analyses. Later on in this Appendix we have
provided readers with a tabulation of all ratings of variables

discussed in this book. Any reader who questions our use of product-moment correlation coefficients in some analysis or set of analyses may refer to our ratings and perform whatever analysis seems to be more appropriate.

We have used the .05 level of statistical significance as a guide, throughout our work, to findings to be taken seriously. This means that we have taken seriously only correlations that are so large that they would have been obtained by chance 5 percent of the time if we repeated our study again and again and if there was actually no relationship between the variables. We are sensitive to a large and growing literature that is critical of the statistical significance test (e.g. Bakan 1966; Labovitz 1970; Lykken 1968; Walster and Cleary 1970), and we have tried to guard against excesses in use of significance tests by working at not capitalizing on chance and by being thoughtful rather than robotic in interpreting our data.

Significance tests may be one-tailed or two-tailed. We used one-tailed tests if we specifically hypothesized that there would be either a positive or a negative relationship between two variables, but not both. Thus, if we predicted a positive correlation between variable A and variable B, we concluded that the correlation should be taken seriously only if it was so large that it would have come from the upper 5 percent of the area of a theoretical distribution of sample correlation coefficients drawn from a universe in which no relationship really existed between the two variables. Two-tailed tests were used in all other instances. In these latter instances, we took a correlation seriously if it was so large that it would come from the lower 2½ percent (a large negative correlation) or upper 2½ percent (a large positive correlation) of the area of a theoretical distribution of correlation coefficients sampled from a universe in which the true correlation was .00. In short, for us the significance test is primarily an indicator of whether a correlation differs enough from no correlation (.00) to be worth taking seriously. Our significance tests provide a rule of thumb for deciding which relationships are potentially of significance (cf. Winch and Campbell 1969).

We should note that statistical significance is related to the number of cases on which a correlation is based. The

greater the number of cases, the smaller the correlation coefficient necessary to give statistical significance. Consequently,
what is a significant correlation varies quite a bit in this
book from analysis to analysis as a result of variations in
the number of cases underlying analyses.

In research in which many measures are made and large
correlation matrices are generated, even if the numerical
data are the result only of random errors, roughly 5 percent
of the obtained correlations will be statistically significant.
The unscrupulous researcher, the ambitious researcher, or
the researcher who is good at self-deception could conceivably
select some of the chance significant correlations, make up
hypotheses to fit them, and then prepare scholarly publications
reporting findings as though the hypotheses had been tested.
Such chance correlations, generated without prior hypotheses,
without the precision of measurement that tends to be present
if one is working from hypotheses, and without the provision
of supplementary hypothesis-probing analyses, are probably
not as likely to be replicated in subsequent research as hypothesis-testing correlations. Furthermore, in selecting analyses
to report, it is possible to bias one's reports so that the correlations that supported one's hypotheses are reported and
those that did not are not. A scholarly report that makes it
seem as though 100 percent of the correlations examined to
test a hypothesis are significant when only 5 percent were
significant would be extremely misleading.

To aid others in the evaluation of the research reported here,
we would like to report what percentage of the hypothesis-
testing statistical analyses that we carried out provided
statistically significant support of our hypotheses and what
percentage did not. But before we do so, we must explain
several things. Many of the hypotheses we started with we
could not test. The data were insufficient to allow for substantial numbers of cases to rate, or the data on each of two
measures to be correlated were so meager that when we came
to computing a correlation coefficient there were insufficient
cases to provide any real test of the hypothesis. Then there
were measures we attempted that seemed inadequate when
we did validity analyses; these measures were too highly
correlated with the wrong things or inadequately correlated

with measures of the same or similar things. Then, too, except for the hypotheses that were stated explicitly in our proposal to the National Institute of Mental Health, we often operated with notions that certain analyses *might* work, or would be interesting to look at, or would not be interesting to look at but might interest others. There were hypotheses that one of us had that the other two of us did not, and there were variables measured simply because some rater thought it might be interesting to measure them. Finally, there were measures and hypotheses in the study which on subsequent reflection (and almost always independently of the results of statistical analysis to test hypotheses about grief and mourning) seemed to be illogical or inappropriate. All in all, there is a wide range of formally written hypotheses, guesses, intuitions, curiosities, and bad ideas that might be called hypotheses by some definitions but not by others. By our definition, a hypothesis is something we believed in enough to write down and agree upon prior to any measure. The question is, then: How many hypothesis-testing statistics were significant and how many were not? The answer seems to be that 34 of 105 were statistically significant. Of the 81 that failed to support hypotheses, 27 are reported in Appendix sections 2.0 and 4.0, and 20 others involved measures of mourning duration and time to remarriage, an area of hypotheses in which we were dead wrong and which we discuss but little in this monograph. Of the remaining 34, 24 involved variables which we theorized might be tie-maintaining, 8 involved final funeral ceremonies, and 2 involved cleansing of widows. These counts seem to us to be accurate, though it should be pointed out that some of the 81 failures to find significant support for hypotheses involved overlap of the categories in which we had poor success. In other words, there is a certain amount of arbitrariness in the categorization of the correlations for which we had poor success.

0.6 Deviant Case Analysis

Among the joys of doing cross-cultural research involving ethnographic materials is that the researcher and other scholars can return to the original materials on which ratings were based. Hence, there is opportunity to check on what has been found and to hunt for further relevant information. Moreover, investigations of a case do not alter the case, as would be true when gathering data directly from warm individuals.

One thing that is facilitated by the availability of ethnographic materials for review is deviant case analysis (Köbben 1967). By "deviant case" we mean a case that seems not to fit one's hypothesis or explanation when the majority of cases do seem to fit the hypothesis or explanation. If a researcher's theoretical analysis is correct, the theory should be able to deal with a deviant case. Upon further study, a deviant case should either be shown to be a case of botched measurement or be shown to make theoretical sense. It can make sense theoretically if it can be shown, for example, to possess functional alternatives to the processes or culture traits hypothesized to be present or to have the problems that the theory being tested suggests cultures should have if they lack such culture traits. For example there are deviant cases in our analysis in Chapter 4 of tie-breaking and widow remarriage. Most of the deviant cases that have widow remarriage but no tie-breaking were found, upon deviant case analysis, to have a form of tie-breaking we had overlooked. One case appeared to have no tie-breaking and to have, as the theory led us to believe, substantial problems for remarried widows. Of course such analyses are after the fact and are not as trustworthy as a theoretical analysis that was generated before the data consistent with theory were obtained. Nonetheless, deviant case analysis seems to us to be of value, and we report deviant case analyses at several places in this book.

1.0 Material for Chapter 1:

The Expression of
Emotion in Bereavement

Among other things, this Appendix provides information about variables discussed throughout the book. The definitions of some of the variables are discussed at length, and lists are provided of raters and interrater correlations for each of the variables. In the lists of raters, each of the eight raters is represented by a number. The raters are numbered as follows:

1. R. Patricia Walsh
2. Merrie Norman Harrison
3. Douglas A. Jackson
4. Elizabeth Syme
5. Richard Walz
6. Elizabeth Skoogberg
7. Paul C. Rosenblatt
8. Teri-Christine Hall

1.1 Are Other Peoples Like Americans?

Measures were made of three classes of emotional behavior, crying (four measures), fear (three measures), and anger-aggression (nineteen measures). Variables, raters, and reliability data are as follows:

Variable	Raters	Interrater Correlation	Number of Cases
1 Crying frequency	2 7	.72	69
2 Crying duration	2 7	.71	37
3 Frequency, male crying	2 3	.65	61
4 Frequency, female crying	2 3	.49	67
5 Frequency, attempted self-injury	2 7	.86	53
6 Frequency, actual self-injury	2 7	.90	52
7 Frequency, male attempted self-injury	2 3	.67	34
8 Frequency, female attempted self-injury	2 3	.65	37
9 Frequency, male actual self-injury	2 3	.72	31
10 Frequency, female actual self-injury	2 3	.63	35
11 Institutionalized attack by widow of something or someone	2 3	.70	20
12 Institutionalized attack by widower of something or someone	2 3	.85	14
13 Widow attacks self, institutionalized	2 3	.75	16
14 Institutionalized attack by adult offspring of deceased	2 3	.86	14
15 Institutionalized attack by adult siblings of deceased	2 3	.89	17
16 Institutionalized attack by parents of deceased	2 3	.87	15
17 Outgroup member institutionlized target	2 3	.77	17

18 Presumed killer institutionalized target	2 3	.63	13
19 Self institutionalized target	2 3	.76	20
20 Somebody institutionalized target	2 3	.57	26
21 Something institutionalized target	2 3	.59	22
22 Something institutionalized target, not a sacrifice	2 3	.65	10
23 Spontaneous aggression after sudden death	2 3	.73	13
24 Fear of ghosts present[1,2]	1 2 5 8	.36	53
25 Degree of fear of ghosts[1,2]	1 2 5 8	.41	47
26 Fear of bodies present[1,2]	1 2 5 8	.37	31

For the anger and aggression variables (11-23), which were all rated present-absent, we were so afaid of losing some of the small amount of statistical power we had that we averaged ratings, counting cases of rater disagreement on presence-absence as intermediate between agreed-upon presence and agreed-upon absence.

Crying

The five societies for which we lack scores on any measure of crying are the Basque, Copper Eskimo, Lapps, Masai, and Vedda. Three of these five societies, the Lapps, Masai, and Vedda, are among the four societies in our sample that were most difficult to rate, as measured by the proportion of the first 118 measures we made in this study on which these societies yielded data. Although the Basque were rated as lacking crying, Basque literature, such as the stories of Pío Baroja (e.g. "The Restlessness of Shanti Andia" and "The Abyss," both translated and published in 1962), suggests that crying is in fact a part of Basque grief. Thus, among the five cases without scores on crying, the Copper Eskimo might be most likely actually to lack crying in bereavement.

It was indicated in Chapter 1 that aggression directed toward self and away from self are related in our data. To be more precise, 58 of the 78 correlations between the two types of anger-aggression are significantly positive; none is negative.

1.2 Sex Differences in Emotionality

Four ratings not listed above are relevant to this section of Chapter 1:

Variable	Raters	Interrater Correlation	Number of Cases
27 Sex difference, crying	2 7	.68	58
28 Sex difference, attempted self-mutilation	2 7	.92	21
29 Sex difference, actual self-mutilation	2 7	.86	19
30 Sex difference, anger and aggression	2 7	.72	13

In order to investigate the possibility that the dynamics of male and female emotionality are different, we tried two procedures. For emotionality variables on which we had separate measures for men and women, we examined whether the two measures were differently related to each of the 132 other variables on which we had data. This analysis employed statistics described by Dunn and Clark (1969). In addition, where we had ratings of degree of sex difference for a particular kind of emotionality, we correlated the sex difference ratings with the other variables in the study. Admittedly, the two types of analysis are blindly empirical. Moreover, we are limited by what our other variables happen to be; the other variables were not measured with the dynamics of sex difference in mind. Using the two procedures, we found that sex differences were associated in roughly a chance number of cases (5 percent) with other variables in the study. And our examination of the other variables that were related to sex differences reveals to us no interesting consistency or patterning. Thus, given the limitations of the analysis, it would seem that the dynamics of male and female emotionality do not differ; only the levels of emotionality differ.

Crying

For the more sensitive, comparative measure of sex differences in crying (a single rating on each society of whether the sexes were equal or unequal in crying frequency) ratings could be made on 58 of the 78 societies in the sample. On that measure a score of 6.00 means that the sexes are rated as being equal; a score of 2.00 means that women appear to the raters to show much more of the behavior than men, and a score of 10.00 means that men appear to show much more of the behavior than women. Actually, the mean of the 58 societies was 4.07, which differs significantly from 6.00 (t=9.11, df=57, two-tailed p<.001). Thus, women cry significantly more frequently than men in bereavement.

Self-Mutilation

Raters judged for each society which sex, if either, more frequently attempted and actually performed self-mutilation in bereavement. Twenty-one cases were rated by both raters on sex difference in frequency of attempted self-injury, using the same scale that was used for the comparative measure of crying frequency. Unfortunately, the measure correlated too strongly with our index of extract adequacy; the more variables on which a society could be rated, the greater the likelihood that women would seem more inclined to self-mutilate than men (r=-.49, N=21, two-tailed p<.05). In other words, the better the description of the society in death-related areas, the more it seems that women attempt to self-mutilate more frequently than men. Because of this potential sign of invalidity, we decided not to try to interpret the data involving this comparative measure.

A comparative measure of frequency of actual self-mutilation could be made on 19 societies, and that measure did not correlate too strongly with the measure of extract adequacy. The mean of the 19 societies was 4.58, which differs significantly from the sexes' equal point of 6.00 (t=2.57, df=18, two-tailed p<.02). Women in these 19 societies average a higher frequency of self-mutilation during bereavement than do men.

Anger and Aggression

For the comparative measure of sex differences in anger and aggression directed at people and things other than self, men were judged to have a significantly higher frequency of anger and aggression than women ($t=6.58$, df=12, two-tailed p<.001).

2.0 Material for Chapter 2:

The Control of Anger and Aggression

Variables first discussed in Chapter 2 are as follows:

Variable	Rater	Interrater Correlation	Number of Cases
31 Importance of ritual specialists, up to and including initial disposal	2 3	.55	56
32 Ritualization, up to and including initial disposal	2 3	.42	73
33 Amount of contact by bereaved with corpse	2 3	.43	65
34 Isolation of widows	6 7	.64	51
35 Isolation of widowers	6 7	.59	46
36 Isolation of adult offspring of deceased	6 7	.53	41
37 Isolation of parent of subadult deceased offspring	6 7	.57	41
38 Marking of widow	2 6	.89	57
39 Marking of widower	2 6	.85	46
40 Marking of adult offspring of deceased	2 6	1.00	36
41 Marking of subadult offspring of deceased	2 6	.80	26
42 Marking duration, parent of subadult deceased offspring	2 6	.72	21

Tests of discriminant validity indicate that the ratings of importance of ritual specialists are entangled with related variables, none of which is as strong in convergent and discriminant validity or in number of ratable cases as the variable "importance of ritual specialists." The other variables that for at least one rater are too strongly correlated with importance of ritual specialists up to and including initial body disposal are measures of the importance of specialists (1) in body preparation (2) at body disposal (3) following initial disposal, and (4) over all occasions and a measure of overall ritualization of initial death-related activities.

The measure of degree of ritualization of funeral activities up to and including initial body disposal fares less well in validity analysis. In particular, it correlates too well with our index of extract adequacy—the proportion of the first 118 measures made in our research for which a society yielded ratings. The more ratings we could make on a society (and presumably the more information that was available to raters), the higher was the score of the society on degree of ritualization of initial funeral activities (r=.32, N=73, two-tailed p<.01). Degree of ritualization may be a mere artifact of amount of information available. Moreover, as the reader can note above, the interrater reliability of the measure of degree of ritualization was rather low. Consequently, there seems to be little point in studying the correlations of degree of ritualization with other variables.

We plotted possible diffusion paths on each of the crucial aggression variables. For cases on which we had ritual specialists ratings, ratings of the presence of institutionalized attack on somebody clustered to a statistically significant extent on a path running from Oceania, north into Asia, and then south through the Americas. However, there is no conclusive evidence for or against the hypothesis that ritual specialists and the absence of attacking somebody diffuse jointly. A joint diffusion analysis, following Method Four of Naroll and D'Andrade (1963), was indeterminate.

All of the measures discussed in Chapter 2 are, of course, based on pooled ratings. For the measures of duration of marking of bereaved parents, of the amount done by ritual specialists, and of degree of ritualization of initial funeral activities, pooling procedures involved simple averaging for each society of the ratings made by the two raters. For the other marking measures and for the isolation measures— all of which were rated present-absent—cases were dropped on which raters disagreed.

2.1 Analyses: Control of Aggression

Ritual Specialists

The median correlation among the 19 measures of anger and aggression exceeds .80. This is not surprising, since some measures are of similar things and some measures are based on similar instructions. Such nonindependence seems to require multivariate procedures, but the different measures of anger and aggression yielded ratings in from 10 to 53 of the 78 societies. Since multivariate statistics generally require data on all measures from all cases used in an analysis and generally require large numbers of cases, multivariate analysis would have little meaning with these data. Consequently, the best course seems to be to present data from the measures on which we have the largest number of cases: somebody is an institutionalized target (which correlates a median of 1.00 with the other measures of anger and aggression) and the measures of male and of female attempted and actual self-mutilation (which correlate at a median of .67 or better with the other measures of anger and aggression).

Table 1. *Anger, Aggression, and Ritual Specialists*

	Importance of Ritual Specialists	
	Correlation	Number of Cases
Somebody Is Institutionalized Target	-.49**	19
Attempted Self-Mutilation, Female	-.23	27
Attempted Self-Mutilation, Male	-.38*	24
Actual Self-Mutilation, Female	-.26	24
Actual Self-Mutilation, Male	-.42*	21

*p<.05, one-tailed test   **p<.025, one-tailed test

Table 1 summarizes the relationships between the key anger and aggression variables and the measure of importance of ritual specialists up to and including initial body disposal. The correlations in Table 1 indicate that ritual specialists tend to be associated with lower levels of anger and aggression. Not all correlations in the table are significant, but the pattern is consistent.

In Table 1, the effect of ritual specialists seems to be more on male self-mutilation than on female self-mutilation. That seems plausible. Male aggression may do more damage, because of greater average male strength and greater male skill at injuring others (Rosenblatt and Cunningham n.d.). Male aggression may be harder to contain, because of strength, hormonal, and socialization differences between the sexes. Consequently, it makes sense that a societal factor which serves to control aggression would be more strongly linked to male aggression than to female aggression. However, this remains speculation, since the correlations involving male aggression are not significantly different from those involving female aggression, and when we look at the other measures we have of sex-specific aggression, those involving widows and widowers, the pattern is not as clear as it is in the self-mutilation data.

Table 2. *Ritual Specialists and Attacks by Widows and Widowers*

	Importance of Ritual Specialists	
	Correlation	*Number of Cases*
Widow Attacks Something	-.53*	12
Widow Attacks Self	-.39	12
Widower Attacks Something	-.48	12

*p< .05, one-tailed test

Table 2 lists the relationships between the ritual specialists measure and attacks by widows and widowers. The pattern of correlations in Table 2 is less clear than that in Table 1 on the relation of ritual to male as compared to female aggression. Although institutionalized attacks by widowers are more strongly related to importance of ritual specialists than are attacks by widows on self, attacks by widows of something are even more strongly related to importance of ritual specialists.

It should be noted that in Table 2 the ritual specialists measure is more strongly related to attacks on things other than self than to attacks on self. In Table 1 there was also a tendency for attacks away from self to be more strongly associated with the ritual specialist measure. This tendency is what is to be expected if one assumes that the ritual specialists are primarily a control on aggression against others.

In Table 2, as in Table 1, the correlations are negative; ritual specialists tend to be associated with reduced expression of anger and aggression. Taken altogether, the data show rather clearly that ritual specialists are associated with lower levels of anger and aggression.

Ritual specialists are, as we report in Chapter 2, more likely to be present and important in large-scale societies with relatively permanent communities. Our measure of the importance of ritual specialists up to and including initial ceremony correlates positively with the measure from the Ethnographic Atlas that is the single best indicator of societal scale—mean size of local community (r=.50, N=47, two-tailed p<.001). Importance of ritual specialists correlates with two other measures we have included in our analyses that are good indicators of relatively permanent communities. One measure is from the Ethnographic Atlas—presence of rules for inheritance of real property. It correlates with importance of ritual specialists .35 (N=45, two-tailed p=.02). The other measure correlated with importance of ritual specialists is temporary or permanent camp abandonment following a typical adult death. The correlation is negative, -.33 (N=48, two-tailed p<.05), which means that where people are more prone to abandon a community site following a death, ritual specialists are less important.

Table 3. *Correlations of Isolation of Mourners with Types of Institutionalized Anger and Aggression*

Attack	Person Isolated							
	Widow		*Widower*		*Adult Offspring*		*Parent*	
	r	N	r	N	r	N	r	N
Widow Attacks Something	.63**	13						
Widow Attacks Self	.95**	10						
Widower Attacks Something			.61*	9				
Adult Offspring Attacks Something					.00	9		
Parent Attacks Something							.00	9
Somebody Is Institutionalized Target	.43	14	.44	14	.27	12	.24	13

*p<.05, one-tailed test

**p<.025, one-tailed test

Note:—The underlined significant correlation hinges on one crucial case.

Table 4. *Correlations of Marking of Mourners with Types of Institutionalized Anger and Aggression*

Attack	Person Marked									
	Widow		Widower		Adult Offspring		Subadult Offspring		Parents	
	r	N	r	N	r	N	r	N	r	N
Widow Attacks Something	.24	16								
Widow Attacks Self	.50*	13								
Widower Attacks Something			.45	6						
Adult Offspring Attacks Something					.09	7				
Parent Attacks Something									.97**	6
Somebody Is Institutionalized Target	.43*	19	.17	13	.21	11	-.50	6	.69	5

*p<.05, one-tailed test
**p<.025, one-tailed test
Note:—The underlined significant correlation hinges on two crucial cases. The measure of marking of parents is a measure of duration; the other marking measures are of simple presence or absence.

Isolation

It can be seen in Table 3 that isolation of widows correlates significantly with the variables: widow attacks either verbally or physically some institutionalized target (including self) and widow attacks self as institutionalized target. Isolation of widowers correlates significantly with widower attacks on some institutionalized target; however, that correlation is less trustworthy, because it hinges on a single case in which isolation is present and there is institutionalized attack by widowers of something. Isolation of adult offspring who are mourning for their own parents does not correlate significantly either with adult offspring attacking some institutionalized target or with the variable somebody is institutionalized target. And isolation of parents who are mourning for subadult offspring does not correlate significantly with parents attacking some institutionalized target or with the variable somebody is institutionalized target.

Marking

As is indicated in Table 4, marking of widows correlates significantly with two measures of institutionalized anger and aggression, the measure of widow attacking self and the measure "somebody is institutionalized target." However, the former correlation is less trustworthy, because it hinges on only two cases in which both self-attack and marking are absent. For parents of a deceased subadult offspring we measured duration of marking, using a five-point scale ranging from absent to present for at least thirty days. This measure was used rather than mere presence-absence, because for parents it gave stronger convergent and discriminant validity. This measure of marking of mourning parents correlates significantly with institutionalized attack on something or somebody by parents of deceased subadult offspring; however, the correlation is based on only six cases. For the other categories of mourner, marking measures are not significantly related to anger and aggression. Even if they were, interpretation of the correlations might be difficult. Marking of both subadult and of adult offspring of the deceased correlates too strongly with our index of extract adequacy, the proportion of the first 118 variables on which each case was ratable.

Our marking and isolation measures are correlated positively for the different categories of bereaved persons (from a low of .22, N=18, which is not significant, for adult offspring of deceased parents to a high of .50, N=20, p<.05 for widowers). Nonetheless, there seems to be some possibility that marking and isolation are partial functional alternatives. This possibility is discussed in Chapter 2.

3.0 Material for Chapter 3:

Ghosts

Variables first discussed in this chapter:

Variable	Raters	Interrater Correlation	Number of Cases
43 Ghosts present[1]	1 2 5 8	.50	64
44 Ghosts perceived are of people best known	2 6	.46	44
45 Eventual distance of spirits[1]	1 2 5 8	.39	44

In studying ghosts, we used material from five randomly chosen societies in our sample—Mbundu, Mende, Todas, Trobriand Islanders, and Tswana—to generate some hypotheses and to develop some of our rating and coding schemas. In order to avoid bias in interpreting data analyses, these societies were not rated on the ghost variables discussed in this chapter. It would not be legitimate to test hypotheses using cases that inspired the hypotheses. Thus, only 73 of societies in the sample are used to examine the hypotheses about ghosts that are discussed in this chapter.

The raters were asked whether or not ghost beliefs, as we defined them, were present in these 73 societies. There were four raters, and we counted ghost beliefs as present or absent in a society if at least three of the raters were in agreement on presence or absence. For 66 societies, three or four raters could agree. In 52 of these 66, agreement was unanimous, and in 9 of the other 14, one rater made no rating and the other three raters were unanimous.

Of the 66 societies for which there was substantial rater agreement on presence or absence of ghost beliefs, ghost beliefs were
rated present in 65. Only the Masai were rated as lacking ghost
beliefs, and the Masai society was next-to-last among our 78
societies in ratability, as measured by the proportion of the
first 118 variables on which it yielded a pooled rating. Moreover, the Arusha, a people closely related to the Masai, seem
to have ghost beliefs as we define them (Gulliver 1964). We
are not, as a consequence, very confident that the Masai really
lack ghost beliefs. We may merely lack adequate information.
Ghost beliefs seem to us to be universal or nearly universal
cross-culturally. This conclusion was drawn years ago by
Frazer (1933-36: 2, ix) and by Simmons (1945: 233); however,
their definitions of ghost were somewhat different from ours
and their methods were rather more casual than ours.

4.0 Material for Chapter 4:

Tie-Breaking and
the Death of a Spouse

Variables first discussed in Chapter 4 and in the discussion of Chapter 4 that appears in this Appendix:

Variable	Raters	Interrater Correlation	Number of Cases
46 Percentage of widowers remarrying	1 7	.41	22
47 Percentage of widowers remarrying by the sororate	7 8	.37	13
48 Sororate present vs. absent	7 8	.69	25
49 Percentage of widows remarrying	1 7	.74	34
50 Percentage of widows remarrying by the levirate	7 8	.61	24
51 Levirate present vs. absent	7 8	1.00	47
52 Disposal, etc., of personal property	2 7	.71	55
53 Useful property destroyed	4 7	.51	71
54 Name taboo present[2]	2 7	.93	46
55 Dwelling or room abandoned	2 7	.82	63

Variable	Raters	Interrater Correlation	Number of Cases
56 Camp or village abandoned	2 7	.65	68
57 Name taboo applies to close relatives	2 7	.86	19
58 Cleansing of widows	1 4	.78	34
59 Ghosts feared those of people best known	2 6	.51	30

There were two problems we faced in carrying out our investigation of remarriage, the problem of independent identification of tie-breaking customs and the problem of definition of remarriage. We had somehow to identify tie-breaking customs independently of their associations with remarriage in our sample of 78 societies. We did this through reading ethnographic reports of societies not in our research sample and making guesses about what seemed to eliminate reminders of deceased persons.

Defining marriage and remarriage for comparative study is notoriously difficult. We were willing, however, to operate with an inelegant working definition in order to get at the psychological and social phenomena of interest. We considered remarriage to be either what the ethnographer called marriage, whether or not a qualifying statement was given (rarely was one given), or a relationship that was both heterosexual and coresidential.

Levirate remarriage was defined as the marriage of a widow to any male member of her deceased husband's family, lineage, or clan; sororate remarriage was defined as marriage of a widower to any member of his deceased wife's family, lineage, or clan. The measures of remarriage were intended to be of actual occurrence; however, it is likely that those ratings are contaminated by norm statements that appeared to be statements about actual behavior.

Name taboos were rated on a three-point continuum, (1) absent (2) present but temporary, and (3) present and permanent. Raters were instructed to use a broad definition of taboo, one that would include in the category of taboo a norm that it is in bad taste to mention the name of the deceased person. The disposal of personal property of the deceased was rated with two items. One item asked for ratings of "some personal utensils or prized objects of typical dead adult disposed of with corpse or given to other groups or put out of sight and use for substantial amount of time." The other assessed destruction of potentially usable personal property of the deceased on a four-point continuum from absent to present but symbolic to present and substantial to present and total. The combined ratings of the two property disposal items correlate with each other .55, N=49, one-tailed p<.0005. Desertion or destruction of the dwelling or a room of the dwelling of the deceased was measured and considered present whether it was present temporarily or permanently. Temporary or permanent camp or village abandonment was the other of the key tie-breaking variables.

Combined ratings of variables reported for the first time in Chapter 4 represent simple adding or averaging of variables with adequate convergent and discriminant validity. For variables rated present-absent by two raters, cases of disagreement were deleted.

When we came to making ratings on widowers, we found that we could get only very low reliabilty and small numbers of cases on two measures that we had to drop, percentage of widowers remarrying and percentage of widowers remarrying by the sororate. The fact that it was easier to get strong measures on widows may be due to the fact that in many ethnographies the material dealing with death is based on the typical scenario followed when an older married man dies.

All twenty correlations between the four remarriage variables and the five tie-breaking variables are positive. However, in six of the twelve statistically significant relationships, there is a crucial case or two that makes the relationship significant. For example we have only two cases in which the sororate was rated as absent. Thus, in the analyses involving presence or absence of sororate, the location of those two cases has a very strong influence on the strength of relationship. As a warning to the reader, we have underlined all the correlations in Table 5 that are significantly different from .00 by a conventional test of significance but which are based on a contingency

Table 5. *Tie-Breaking Customs and Remarriage*

	Levirate Present		Percent of Widows Who Remarry		Percent Levirate Marriage		Sororate Present		Fear of Ghosts Present		Degree of Fear of Ghosts	
	r	N	r	N	r	N	r	N	r	N	r	N
Disposal of Personal Objects	.56**	33	.14	21	.56*	15	.79**	20	.19	28	.38**	28
Useful Property Destroyed	.45**	43	.41**	32	.80**	21	.60**	22	-.04	42	.07	40
Name Taboo Present	.38*	29	.11	18	.51*	14	.28	15	-.37*	25	-.42**	24
Dwelling or Room Abandoned	.08	31	.35*	25	.44**	15	.29	19	.10	34	.19	33
Camp or Village Abandoned	.11	34	.16	25	.50*	16	.09	18	.01	34	.02	33
Fear of Ghosts Present	.35*	28	.68**	19	.48*	18	.68**	17				
Degree of Fear of Ghosts	.16	28	.58**	17	.10	18	.58**	17				

*p<.05, one-tailed test   **p<.01, one-tailed test   Note:—Underlined significant correlations hinge on one or two crucial cases.

table that has only one or two cases in a crucial cell. The evidence is not as strong as one might wish, but it seems to indicate that tie-breaking customs facilitate remarriage.

The disposal of the property of the deceased and the destruction of the house could, of course, be linked with beliefs that the deceased needs those things in an afterworld. However, in our sample there are a number of peoples with that sort of belief who fail to destroy property of the deceased. Instead, they bury toylike replicas of needed objects, destroy property too worn to use, or perform a ceremony over some useful objects that somehow transfers their essence to an afterworld. Thus, there is no necessary requirement that useful personal property of the deceased be disposed of with the deceased in order for the property to be of use to the deceased in an afterworld.

An interesting perspective on the function of name taboos comes from a consideration of the Tikopia. Among the Tikopia, "This prohibition against speaking the name of the parent is in force primarily while they live; the *tapu* is lifted on their death, and many a son or daughter utters for the first time the name of father or mother in the *tani soa*, the funeral dirge which is sung over the corpse [Firth 1936: 182]." It may be that the typical name taboo practice cross-culturally—one of not uttering the name of a deceased person—helps to obliterate reminders of the deceased, but the Tikopian practice seems as good as the standard taboo at signifying that things have changed and that the old behavior is no longer appropriate. Both in Tikopia and in societies practicing the more common taboo, the *change* in naming practice can be expected to facilitate adjustment to the death by promoting new patterns of response to old stimuli.

4.1 Ghost Fear and Remarriage

Among the ratings made on ghosts was a measure of whether the ghosts that people feared were of people they knew best. (In Chapter 3 we discussed whether the ghosts that people *perceive* are of those they knew best.) If ghost fear serves tie-breaking functions, then the ghosts that people fear should be of people who, when alive, were best known to them. In twenty of the twenty-three cases that could be rated with agreement by both raters, people feared most the ghosts of people they knew best. These data may provide some additional support for the contention that ghost fear serves tie-breaking functions, though the finding may be at least in part an artifact of the relatively high frequency with which ghosts of familiar people are the ones that people perceive.

5.0 Material for Chapter 5:

Ceremonies

Variables first discussed in Chapter 5 and in the Appendix materials dealing with Chapter 5 are as follows:

Variable	Raters	Interrater Correlation	Number of Cases
60 Attendance, initial ceremonies	3 8	.50	68
61 Attendance, final ceremonies	3 8	.66	32
62 Mourning duration, widowers	2 7	.81	36
63 Mourning duration, widows	2 7	.70	48
64 Mourning duration, adult offspring	2 7	.72	17
65 Final ceremonies, present or absent[1]	2 3 7 8	.62	67
66 Series of final ceremonies, yes or no	3 8	.62	38
67 Final ceremony coincides with annual death ceremonies, yes or no	3 8	.45	40
68 Final disposal of remains at final ceremony, yes or no	3 8	.56	40
69 Final ceremony terminates mourning, yes or no	3 8	.63	33

Variable	Raters	Interrater Correlation	Number of Cases
70 Amount of grief after end of mourning	2 7	.75	23
71 Mourning duration, widowers	2 7	.81	36
72 Mourning duration, widows	2 7	.70	48
73 Feasting at initial ceremonies, yes or no	1 2	.81	55
74 Games at initial ceremonies, yes or no	1 2	.77	39
75 Dances at initial ceremonies, yes or no	1 2	.95	43
76 Sexual liberties at initial ceremonies, yes or no	1 2	1.00	17
77 Alcohol at intial ceremonies, yes or no	1 2	.90	39
78 Feasting at final ceremonies, yes or no	· 1 2	1.00	33
79 Games at final ceremonies, yes or no	1 2	.60	16
80 Dances at final ceremonies, yes or no	1 2	.82	24
81 Sexual liberties at final ceremonies, yes or no	1 2	1.00	9
82 Alcohol at final ceremonies, yes or no	1 2	.79	21
83 Final ceremony held for more than one death at a time, yes or no	1 2	.83	21

5.1 Results: Grief and Final Ceremonies

The global measure of grief after the end of mourning correlated -.53 (N=15, p<.025, one-tailed test) with the presence of final ceremonies. Thus, as was hypothesized, final ceremonies seem to serve to time-limit grief.

The presence vs. absence of final ceremonies is not significantly correlated with any of our measures of mourning duration. For widows, the correlation is -.08, N=38; for widowers, it is .05, N=28; and for adult offspring mourning the death of a parent, it is .31, N=13. For widows and widowers, however, mourning duration is longer where the final ceremony is present and terminates mourning (for widows the correlation is .52, N=23, two-tailed probability of chance occurrence is approximately .01; for widowers the correlation is .46, N=16, two-tailed p<.10). Moreover, societies with longer mourning duration for widows and widowers are less likely to have grief after the end of mourning (r=-.58, N=15, two-tailed p<.05 for widows and r=-.72, N=13, two-tailed p<.01 for widowers). These statistically significant correlations suggest that final ceremonies may seem to terminate grief after the end of mourning because of an artifact of longer mourning duration where final ceremonies terminate mourning or because a longer mourning duration allows working through to occur adequately. But the case for the alternative interpretation is weakened by the failure of mourning duration to be significantly associated with the presence or absence of final ceremonies.

5.2 Ceremony Attendance and Time-Limiting of Grief

The data we have that bear on the issue of attendance at ceremonies is a correlation based on only seven cases and hence very untrustworthy. The measure of attendance at final ceremonies for adults correlates negatively with grief after the end of mourning (r=-.68, p<.05, one-tailed test). What this finding suggests is that among societies with final ceremonies, the greater the attendance at final ceremonies, the more effectively do final ceremonies terminate grief. Although this one correlation constitutes anything but compelling evidence, it is consistent with the hypothesis that effective time-limiting of mourning involves ceremonies attended by substantial numbers of people.

5.3 Attendance Inducements

In order to find out whether attendance promotion devices work it seems necessary to control somehow for the number of people available to attend ceremonies. It would be meaningless to correlate presence-absence of an attendance promotion device with attendance, lumping together societies in which only 10 kinfolk were within a day's travel of a funeral ceremony with societies in which 400 kinfolk were within a day's travel of a funeral ceremony. We therefore devised an index of the proportion of local group attending ceremonies. The index was produced by dividing our ratings of number of people attending a given kind of ceremony by the ratings in the Ethnographic Atlas of mean size of local community. In using the Ethnographic Atlas ratings, we combined the four largest categories of community size into a single category, 400 or more people. We did this on the assumption that acquaintance groups were unlikely to exceed 400 persons for the typical bereaved or deceased adult.

The index of proportion of local group in attendance at final ceremonies for adult dead is significantly correlated with two of our six measures of inducements to attend final ceremonies—holding ceremonies for more than one death at a time ($r=.59$, $N=10$, one-tailed $p<.05$) and sex liberties at final ceremonies for deceased adults ($r=.75$, $N=7$, one-tailed $p<.05$). Both correlations are based on such a small number of cases that they must be interpreted with extreme caution. The index of proportion of local group attending initial ceremonies for adult dead correlates significantly with none of our five measures of inducements to attend initial ceremonies.

To explore further the possible usefulness of inducements to attend ceremonies we examined the relationship, for societies with ghost fear and with body fear, between inducements and our indexes of proportion of local group attending ceremonies. It seems reasonable to expect that inducements might make the greatest difference in societies with deterrents to attend ceremonies. Ghost fear seems a possible deterrent to attend both initial and final ceremonies, body fear a deterrent to attend at least initial ceremonies. Unfortunately, unratable cases on our indexes of attendance, in our measures of inducements, and in our measures of fear combine to make for very small numbers of cases in analyses combining all three kinds of variables. Thus, the analyses are at best suggestive of possible relationships.

For societies with fear of body and data on attendance at

initial ceremonies, only three inducements to attend initial ceremonies have any variability—feasts, dances, and games. Correlations are, of course, impossible if one variable being correlated has no variability. The analyses involving each of the three inducements to attend initial ceremonies are based on only three or four cases, but for each inducement the direction of relationship with the index of proportion of local group in attendance at initial ceremonies is positive.

For societies with fear of ghosts and data on attendance at initial ceremonies, only four inducements to attend initial ceremonies have any variability—feasts, dances, alcohol, and games. Two of the four inducements are associated positively with our index of proportion of local group in attendance at initial ceremonies. The relationships are based on from fourteen to twenty-one cases, and no relationship is strong.

For societies with fear of ghosts and data on attendance at final ceremonies, only four inducements to attend final ceremonies have variability—dances, alcohol, games, and holding ceremonies for more than one person at a time. The relationship between each of the four inducements to attend final ceremonies and our index of proportion of local group in attendance at final ceremonies is based on from three to seven cases. Three of the four correlations are positive, but none is statistically significant. Thus we have insufficient justification for a conclusion that inducements work but too much suggestive data to forget the idea. With more cases, more sensitive attendance measures, and with examination of the role of other attendance deterrents, such as bad weather or difficulty of travel, the hypothesis that inducements work would receive a stronger winnowing.

6.0 Material for Chapter 6:

The Effect of
Christianity on Death Customs

The variables discussed for the first time in this chapter and not in the Ethnographic Atlas are as follows:

Variable	Raters	Interrater Correlation	Number of Cases
84 Christian influence	1 7	.92	78
85 Belief in adult rein- carnation present	1 4	.87	62
86 Conflict and resentment over inheritance	4 7	.51	20
87 Female age of marriage	1 4	.97	42

Twenty-seven of the seventy-eight societies in the sample were rated as having at least some Christian influence, and two of these societies were rated as being entirely Christian. Christian influence is associated in our sample with the Ethnographic Atlas ratings of mean size of local communities (r=.32, N=67, two-tailed p<.01), and with the Atlas ratings of the combined importance of animal husbandry and agriculture as a source of calories (r=.27, N=78, two-tailed p<.02).

The correlation between degree of Christian influence and belief in adult reincarnation is -.26, N=62, two-tailed p<.05. Christian influence is associated with substantially greater conflict and resentment over the inheritance of property (r=.49, N=20, two-tailed p<.05), with substantially less property destruction (r=-.25, N=71, two-tailed p<.05), and with the presence of inheritance rules for real (as opposed to movable) property (r=.42, N=59, two-tailed p<.001).

In the data dealing with women, Christian influence is associated with a lower level of polygyny in the Ethnographic Atlas ratings (r=-.20, N=77, two-tailed p<.10) and with an older age of marriage for females (r=.34, N=42, two-tailed p<.05). For widows, Christianity is associated with a longer mourning duration (r=.32, N=48, two-tailed p<.05), with a lower percentage of remarriage by the levirate (r=-.35, N=24, two-tailed p<.10), with less isolation (r=-.31, N=40, two-tailed p<.05), and with less cleansing during death ceremonies (r=.37, N=34, two-tailed p<.05).

7.0 Code Book

Eighty-seven variables for which we made ratings were discussed in this book and listed in the Appendix. Here we present a brief description of how each of these eighty-seven variables was scored. Following the Code Book, we list in a Ratings Table the scores of each society on all but two of the eight-seven variables. We dropped two variables from the Code Book because they did not survive initial validity analysis (variables 46 and 47). For some variables, the total number of cases with data in the Ratings Table differs from the totals listed in the Appendix. The numbers in the Appendix are for interrater reliability correlations. For some variables, cases of rater disagreement were deleted in pooling ratings to yield the data used in hypothesis tests and listed in the Ratings Table. Note that the scores in the Ratings Table represent judgments, not concrete reality, and must be interpreted with caution. For example our ratings of percentage of widows remarrying may all be in error, though the societies may be ordered with considerable accuracy relative to one another.

Variable 1. Crying frequency. Scores range from 0 (crying is absent) to 8 (crying is very frequent).

Variable 2. Crying duration. Scores range from 0 (less than a few minutes) to 16 (more than a week).

Variable 3. Frequency, male crying. Scores range from 00 (absent) to 10 (always occurs).

Variable 4. Frequency, female crying. Scores range from 00 (absent) to 10 (always occurs).

Variable 5. Frequency, attempted self-injury. Scores range from 0 (absent) to 8 (very frequent).

Variable 6. Frequency, actual self-injury. Scores range from 0 (absent) to 8 (very frequent).

Variable 7. Frequency, male attempted self-injury. Scores range from 00 (absent) to 10 (occurs always).

Variable 8. Frequency, female attempted self-injury. Scores range from 00 (absent) to 10 (occurs always).

Variable 9. Frequency, male actual self-injury. Scores range from 00 (absent) to 10 (occurs always).

Variable 10. Frequency, female actual self-injury. Scores range from 00 (absent) to 10 (occurs always).

Variable 11. Institutionalized attack by widow of something or someone. Scores range from 0 (both raters say it is absent) to 2 (both raters say it is present).

Variable 12. Institutionalized attack by widower of something or someone. Scoring same as for variable 11.

Variable 13. Institutionalized attack on self by widow. Scoring same as for variable 11.

Variable 14. Institutionalized attack by adult offspring of deceased. Scoring same as for variable 11.

Variable 15. Institutionalized attack by adult offspring of deceased. Scoring same as for variable 11.

Variable 16. Institutionalized attack by adult siblings of deceased. Scoring same as for variable 11.

Variable 17. Outgroup member institutionalized target. Scoring same as for variable 11.

Variable 18. Presumed killer institutionalized target. Scoring same as for variable 11.

Variable 19. Self-institutionalized target. Scoring same as for variable 11.

Variable 20. Somebody institutionalized target. Scoring same as for variable 11.

Variable 21. Something institutionalized target. Scoring same as for variable 11.

Variable 22. Something institutionalized target, not a sacrifice. Scoring same as for variable 11.

Variable 23. Spontaneous aggression after sudden death. Scoring same as for variable 11.

Variable 24.   Fear of ghosts present. Scores are 0 (absent) and 1 (present).

Variable 25.   Degree of fear of ghosts. Scores range from 00 (none) to 30 (terror).

Variable 26.   Fear of bodies present. Scores are 0 (absent) and 1 (present).

Variable 27.   Sex difference, crying. Scores range from 2 (women show more crying than men) through 6 (sexes approximately equal) to 9 (men show more crying than women).

Variable 28.   Sex difference, attempted self-mutilation. Scores range from 02 (women show much more of it than men) through 06 (sexes approximately equal) to 10 (men show much more of it than women).

Variable 29.   Sex difference, actual self-mutilation. Scores range from 02 (women show much more of it than men) through 06 (sexes approximately equal) to 10 (men show much more of it than women).

Variable 30.   Sex difference, anger and aggression. Scores range from 1 (sexes equal) to 5 (men show much more of the behavior).

Variable 31.   Importance of ritual specialists up to and including initial body disposal. Scores range from 00 (specialists do nothing) to 10 (everything or almost everything is done by specialists).

Variable 32.   Ritualization up to and including initial disposal. Scores range from 0 (none) to 8 (a very large amount).

Variable 33.   Amount of contact by bereaved with corpse. Scores range from 0 (none) to 8 (a very great deal).

Variable 34.   Isolation of widows. Scores are 0 (absent) and 1 (present).

Variable 35.   Isolation of widowers. Scores are 0 (absent) and 1 (present).

Variable 36.   Isolation of adult offspring of deceased. Scores are 0 (absent) and 1 (present).

Variable 37.   Isolation of parent of deceased subadult offspring. Scores are 0 (absent) and 1 (present).

Variable 38.   Marking of widows. Scores are 0 (absent) and 1 (present).

Variable 39. Marking of widowers. Scoring same as for variable 38.

Variable 40. Marking of adult offspring of deceased. Scoring as for variable 38.

Variable 41. Marking of subadult offspring of deceased. Scoring same as for variable 38.

Variable 42. Marking duration, parent of subadult offspring. Scores range from 0 (absent) to 4 (present for at least thirty days).

Variable 43. Ghosts present. Scored 0 (no) and 1 (yes).

Variable 44. Ghosts perceived are of those best known. Scored 0 (no) and 1 (yes).

Variable 45. Eventual distance of spirits. Scores range from 00 (close to survivors) to 20 (always far away from survivors).

Variable 46. Percentage of widowers remarrying. Not included in Ratings Table.

Variable 47. Percentage of widowers remarrying by the sororate. Not included in the Ratings Table.

Variable 48. Sororate present vs. absent. Scored 0 (absent) and 1 (present).

Variable 49. Percentage of widows remarrying. Scores are the sum of estimates by two raters and range from 000 to 200.

Variable 50. Percentage of widows remarrying by the levirate. Scores range from 00 to 99.

Variable 51. Levirate present vs. absent. Scores are 0 (absent) and 1 (present).

Variable 52. Some personal objects of deceased are disposed of with corpse or given to other groups or put out of sight and use for a substantial amount of time. Scores are 0 (no) and 1 (yes).

Variable 53. Amount of useful property destroyed. Scores range from 00 (none) to 12 (most complete amount of property destroyed).

Variable 54. Name taboo present. Scores range from 0 (no name taboo) to 4 (name taboo present and permanent).

Variable 55. Dwelling or room of deceased abandoned at least temporarily. Scores are 0 (no) and 1 (yes).

Variable 56. Temporary or permanent camp or village abandonment. Scores are 0 (no) and 1 (yes).

Variable 57. Name taboo, if present, applies primarily to close relatives or behavior in presence of close relatives of the deceased. Scores are 0 (no) and 1 (yes).

Variable 58. Cleansing of widows. Scores range from 0 (absent) to 4 (definitely present).

Variable 59. Ghosts feared those of people best known. Scores are 0 (no) and 1 (yes).

Variable 60. Attendance, initial funeral ceremonies. Scores range from 000 to 999, with all numbers above 999 counted as 999.

Variable 61. Attendance, final funeral ceremonies. Scores range from 000 to 999, with all numbers above 999 counted as 999.

Variable 62. Mourning duration, widowers. Scores could range from 000 days to 999 days, with longer durations counted as 999 days.

Variable 63. Mourning duration, widows. Scores could range from 000 days to 999 days, with longer durations counted as 999 days.

Variable 64. Mourning duration, adult offspring. Scores could range from 000 days to 999 days, with longer durations counted as 999 days.

Variable 65. Final ceremonies present or absent. Scored as 0 (absent) and 1 (present).

Variable 66. Series of final ceremonies. Scored as 0 (no) and 1 (yes).

Variable 67. Final ceremony coincides with annual death ceremonies. Scored as 0 (no) and 1 (yes).

Variable 68. Final disposal of remains at final ceremony. Scored as 0 (no) and 1 (yes).

Variable 69. Final ceremony terminates mourning. Scored as 0 (no) or 1 (yes).

Variable 70. Amount of grief after end of mourning. Scores range from 0 (absent) to 8 (extremely significant).

Variable 71. Mourning duration, widowers. Scores range

from 000 days to 999 days, with durations above 999 days counted as 999 days.

Variable 72. Mourning duration, widows. Scores range from 000 days to 999 days, with durations above 999 days counted as 999 days.

Variable 73. Feasting at initial funeral ceremonies. Scored 0 (absent) and 1 (present).

Variable 74. Games at initial funeral ceremonies. Scored 0 (absent) and 1 (present).

Variable 75. Dances at initial funeral ceremonies. Scored 0 (absent) and 1 (present).

Variable 76. Sexual liberties at initial funeral ceremonies. Scored 0 (absent) and 1 (present).

Variable 77. Alcohol at initial funeral ceremonies. Scored 0 (absent) and 1 (present).

Variable 78. Feasting at final funeral ceremonies. Scored 0 (absent) and 1 (present).

Variable 79. Games at final funeral ceremonies. Scored 0 (absent) and 1 (present).

Variable 80. Dances at final funeral ceremonies. Scored 0 (absent) and 1 (present).

Variable 81. Sexual liberties at final ceremonies. Scored 0 (absent) and 1 (present).

Variable 82. Alcohol at final ceremonies. Scored 0 (absent) and 1 (present).

Variable 83. Final ceremony held for more than one death at a time. Scored 0 (no) and 1 (yes).

Variable 84. Degree of Christian influence. Scores range from 00 (none) to 80 (entirely Christian).

Variable 85. Belief in reincarnation of deceased adults. Scores range from 0 (absent) to 4.

Variable 86. Conflict and resentment over property inheritance. Scores range from 0 (none) to 8.

Variable 87. Age of marriage, females. Scores are in years and tenths of years.

8.0 Ratings Table

This table contains ratings pooled across two or more raters for eighty-seven variables discussed in this book and listed in the Appendix and Code Book. The ratings for Variables 46 and 47 were not pooled, because the ratings of these variables by the individual raters seemed inadequate in an initial validity analysis; hence we omit those two variable numbers in this table. In this table a dot (.) means that there is no pooled rating for a given society on a given variable.

Society	1	2	3	4	5	6	7	8	9	10	11-21
01 Abipone	8	16	00	09	.	.	00	00	00	00	. . . . 2 2
02 Ainu	6	.	.	.	.	.	1	1	.	.	. . . .
03 Andamanese	8	.	.	09	09	0	0	00	00	00	00
04 Aweikoma	8	16	08	08	0	0	00	00	00	00	. . . . . 2 . . 2 2
05 Azande	8	.	.	07	08	8	.	00	06	00	03
06 Balinese	0	.	.	00	00	.	.	00	00	00	00
07 Thai villagers	8	.	.	.	.	.	.	.	.	.	.
08 Basque	.	.	.	.	.	.	0	0	.	.	. . . .
09 Carib	7	.	.	08	08	0	0	00	00	00	00
10 Chinese villagers	8	14	00	08	0	0	00	00	00	00	
11 Chippewa	6	.	.	07	07	3	3	03	03	03	03
12 Comanche	8	.	.	06	09	6	6	05	07	05	07
13 Copper Eskimo	.	.	.	.	.	.	.	.	.	.	0 0 0 0 0 0 0 0 0 0 0
14 Cubeo	8	16	10	10	0	0	00	00	00	00	2 . . 2 . . . 2 . 2 .
15 Eastern Timbira	8	12	09	09	5	4	00	07	00	05	. . . . . 2 . . 2 .
16 Egyptian Fellahin	8	16	09	10	7	7	00	07	00	06	1 0 1 . 1 . . . 1 . .
17 Eyak	.	.	.	05	05	.					
18 Ganda	8	.	.	08	08	0	0	.	.	04	. . . . 2 .
19 Garo	7	.	.	.	.	08	.				 1
20 Gheg	8	.	.	10	10	8	8	06	00	06	00
21 Gros Ventre	8	12	08	08	5	4	04	05	04	05	2 . 2 . 2 . 2 . 2 2 .
22 Haitians	8	.	.	09	09	0	0	.	.	.	.
23 Hausa	7	.	.	06	08	3	1	00	00	00	00
24 Hidatsa	8	12	10	10	8	8	08	08	08	08	. . . 2 . 2 . 2 2 .
25 Hill Maria Gond	8	08	.	.	10	.					
26 Huron	8	16	00	08	0	0	.	.	.	.	. . . . . 2 . . 2 .
27 Ibo	8	14	05	10	3	2	00	02	00	01	2 . 2 . . 2 . . 2 . 2
28 Ifugao	8	.	.	01	09	4	4	02	03	02	03	 2

Society	1	2	3	4	5	6	7	8	9	10	11-21
29 Japanese	.	. .	03	03	0	0	00	00	. .	. .	0 0 0 0 0 0 0 0 0 0 0
30 Javanese	2	02	01	02	0	0	00	00	00	00	0 0 0 0 0 0 0 0 0 0 0
31 Jivaro	.	. . .	09	4	1	01	03	. .	. .		2 2 . . . . . 2 . 2 .
32 Kafa	8	12	09	09	8	8	09	09	09	09	. . . .
33 Kapauku	8	14	08	. .	3	1	02	. .	. .	. .	. . . .
34 Kaska	8	16	06	09	2	2	. .	. .	02	02	. . . .
35 Katab	8	. .	07	10	.						. . . .
36 Klamath	8	. .	10	10	.						. . . .
37 Koreans	8	. .	09	09	.					. .	0 0 0 0 0 0 0 0 0 0 0
38 Lapps											. . . .
39 Lepcha	6										 1
40 Lolo	.	. .	10	10	.						. . . .
41 Manus	8									. .	 2
42 Marshallese	8	. .	06	09							1 . . 1 . 1 . . . 1 .
43 Masai											. . . .
44 Mbundu	8	14	. .	05	0	0				. .	. . . .
45 Mbuti	8	12	05	08	4	3	02	02	01	01	. . . . 2 . 2 .
46 Mende	8	10	. .	09							. . . . 2 2 .
47 Micmac	8	14	05	09	3	2				. .	. 1 . . . 1 . . 1 .
48 Miskito	8	12	00	10	6	2	. .	09	. .	04	2 . 2 . . . . 2 . . .
49 Murngin	8	16	. .	09	8	7	04	07	. .	07	. . . 2 2 2 2 . 2 2 .
50 Nicobarese	8	. .	05	07	.					. .	 2
51 Burmese villagers	7	08	00	06	0	0	00	00	00	00	0 0 0 0 0 0 0 0 0 0 0
52 Omaha	8	16	10	10	8	8	10	10	10	10	2 2 2 2 2 2 2 . 2 2 .
53 Orokaiva	8	12	09	10	8	8	08	09	07	08	2 2 2 2 2 2 . . 2 . .
54 Papago	8	12	08	09						. .	. . . .
55 Pawnee	7	. .	08	08	8	8	06	02	06	02	. . . . . . 2 . 2 2 .
56 Samoans	8	10	08	08	8	8	08	08	08	08	. . . . 2 . . .
57 Santal	8	. .	00	07	.					. .	0 0 0 0 0 0 1
58 Semang	8	12	07	07	.						. . . .
59 Seniang	8	12	05	10	7	7	. .	07	. .	07	2 . 2 . . 2 . . 2 . 2
60 Shavante	8	12	10	10	1	1					. . . .
61 Shilluk	7	. .	05	09	.						 2
62 Siriono	7	. .	00	08	0	0	05	05	05	05	 2
63 Siwans	8	12	. .	09	4	4	. .	04	. .	04	1 0 1 0 0 0 . . 1 . 1
64 Thonga	8	. .	09	09	0	0					 2
65 Tikopia	7	. .	. .		7	7					. . . .
66 Toda	8	. .	10	10	0	0					. . . .
67 Trobrianders	8	16	08	09	0	0					. . . .
68 Trukese	8	. .	05	09	.						. . . .
69 Tswana	8	. .	00	08	0	0					. . . .
70 Tupinamba	8	16	07	07	0	0				. .	. . . . 2 . . 2 .
71 Twana	8	15	09	09	0	0	02	02	02	02	. . . . 1 . 1 .
72 Vanua Levu Fijians	8	. .	08	08							0 0 0 0 0 0 1
73 Vedda											. . . .
74 Walbiri	8	12	08	10	8	8	07	10	07	10	2 2 2 2 2 2 . 2 2 2 .
75 Western Apache	8	. .	10	10	0	0					. . . .
76 Wukchumni	8	14	10	10	0	0				. .	. . . .
77 Yurok	8	16	09	09	0	0	02	02	02	02	. . . . . . 1 1 . 1 .
78 Zapotec	8	12	08	08	0	0				. .	. . . .

Society   *Variable*

	22-27	28-30	31	32-44	45	48-52
01	. 2 2	 1	04	5 3 0 . . . 1 1 1 . . 1 .	. .	 1
02	. . 1 17 . 6	 3	02	4 6 1 1 . . 1 1 . . . 1 2	15	. . . . . 1 1
03	. . 1 17 . 6	 4	00	4 6 . . . . 1 1 1 . . 1 .	10	1 . . . 77 1 1
04	. 2 1 25 . 5	. . . . . .	. .	6 . 1 1 0 0 . . 0 0 . 1 2	08	1 150 60 1 1
05	. . . . 0 4	02 . . .	06	7 7 1 1 . . 1 1 . 8 1 2	07	. . . . . 1 1
06	. . . . . .	. . . . . .	07	7 6 . . . 1 1 1 1 . 1 2		. . . .
07	. . . . 0 .	. . . . .	05	6 7 0 0 0 0 . . . . 2 1 .	13	. . . .
08	. . 0 00 0 2	. . . . .	07	6 5 . . . 0 1 1 1 1 4 1 1	20	0 . . . 00 0 0
09	. . 0 000 .	. . . . .	. .	3 . . . . 0 0 0 0 0 1 .	00	. . . .
10	. . 1 08 . 2	. . . . .	02	5 7 . . . 1 1 1 1 . 1 .	. .	. . . . . 1 .
11	. . . . . .	. . . . .	01	4 5 . . 0 0 1 1 . 1 8 1 .	20	. 175 . . 1 1
12	. . 1 15 . 3	04 04 .	. .	2 5 . . . . 1 1 1 . . 1 .	17	1 155 63 1 1
13	0 0 1 25 . .	. . . . .	00	. . . . 1 1	10	 1
14	. . 0 00 . 4	02 . . 2	01	6 5 0 0 0 0 0 0 0 0 . 1 .	08	. 040 . . . .
15	 4	. 02 .	. .	4 6 1 1 1 0 1 . . . 1 2	05	0 0
16	. . . . 0 3	02 02 .	08	5 4 . . . 0 1 . 1 . . 1 2	. .	 0
17	. . . . 1 .	. . . . .	. .	3 1 . . . 1 1 1 . . 1 2	. .	 1
18	. . 1 12 0 .	. . . . .	00	4 6 . 0 . . 1 1 . . . 1 1	05	. 105 . . . .
19	 2	. . . . .	00	4 7 . 0 . . . . 1 .	17	1 126 . . 1 0
20	. . . . . .	09 09 .	. .	3 4 . . . . 1 .	12	. 175 62 1 .
21	. . . . 0 5	05 05 .	. .	2 4 1 1 0 1 1 1 1 . . 1 .	15	. 160 . . 1 1
22	. . 1 22 . 6	. . . . .	08	5 5 0 0 0 0 1 1 1 1 0 1 2	20	. . . .
23	. . 1 10 1 5	. . . . .	05	3 4 . . 0 0 1 1 . . . 1 .	17	. 155 . . . 0
24	. . . . . .	04 04 .	00	3 5 . . . . 1 . . . . . 1 .	15	1 120 . . 1 1
25	. . 1 12 . 2	. . . . .	01	4 3 0 0 0 . . . . . . 1 .	20	. . . . 73 1 1
26	 2	. . . . .	. .	5 . 1 1 . . 1 1 . . . 1 .	15	 1
27	 2	02 02 .	01	4 5 1 . 0 0 1 1 1 1 . 1 2	15	 0
28	. . 1 22 . 2	05 05 2	05	7 6 1 1 . 1 1 1 1 1 7 1 .	20	. . . .
29	0 0	. . . . .	05	8 6 0 0 0 0 1 1 1 . 1 1	08	 1
30	0 0 1 12 . 6	. . . . .	05	6 7 . 0 0 0 0 0 0 0 1 .	13	. 110 . . . 0
31	. . 1 20 . 2	 3	00	2 6 0 0 0 0 1 . . . . 1 1	. .	. 190 70 1 1
32	. . 0 00 0 6	06 06 .	01	4 6 0 0 0 0 1 1 1 1 . . .	. .	. 095 . . 1 .
33	. . 1 . . .	08 . . .	. .	3 6 0 . . . . 1 2	. .	. 160 . . . .
34	. . 1 20 0 3	. . . . .	. .	2 3 . . . 1 1 1 1 8 1 2	10	1 140 . . 1 1
35	 4	. . . . .	03	4 . . . . 1 0	. .	. 140 45 1 .
36	. . 1 23 . 6	. . . . .	00	2 . 1 1 0 . 1 1 1 . . 1 0	20	1 . . . . 1 1
37	0 0 . . . 4	. . . . .	06	5 3 . . . 1 1 1 1 2 1 .	. .	. 055 . . . .
38	. . 1 . . 1	. . . . .	. .	. . . . 1 2	20	. 165 . . . .
39	1 1 1 20 . .	. . . . .	09	6 5 0 0 0 0 1 1 1 1 0 1 2	. .	1 180 65 1 1

```
Society                        Variable
     22-27    28-30  31          32-44              45    48-52
40  . . 1 22 .  . . . . .  05   7 4 . . . . . . . . . . 1 .  20  . 200 70 1 .
41  . . 1 25 . 5  . . . . 5 04  4 5 1 . . . . . . . . 1 1  05  1 105 00 0 .
42  . . 1 22 . 3  . . . . .  03 4 7 0 0 0 0 . . . . . 1 .  13  1 . . . 10 1 .
43  . . . . . . .  . . . . .  .  1 1 . . . . 1 1 1 1 . 0 . . . . . . . . . 1
44  . . . . . 2  . . . . .  03  6 8 1 . . . 1 0 . . . . 2 . . . . . . . . 1
45  . . 0 00 0 4  04 04 . 00   5 3 0 0 0 0 1 . . . . 1 .  13  . . . . . . . .
46  . . . . . 6  . . . . .  .   4 . 1 1 . . 1 1 . . . . . . . . . . . . . .
47  . . . . . 5  03 . . 5  04  5 4 . 0 . . . . . . . 1 2  . . . 100 . . 1 1
48  . . 1 23 . 2  02 02 .  .   3 6 . . . . 1 . . . . 1 2  17 1 . . . 70 1 1
49  . . 1 13 . 2  03 03 5  04  7 7 . . . . . . . . . 1 2  03 1 197 94 1 .
50  2 2 1 20 . 4  . . . . .  01 7 5 . . . . . . . . . 1 2  15  . . . . . . 1
51  0 0 . . . 2  . . . . .  06 7 3 0 0 0 0 0 0 0 0 . 1 2  . . . . . . . .
52  . . . . . .  . . 08 5  .   2 . . . . . . . . . . 1 0  13 1 090 . . 1 1
53  . . 1 20 0 3  05 05 . . .   4 7 1 1 0 . 1 1 . . 1 2  02 . . . . 54 1 1
54  . . 1 20 1 5  . . . .  00  2 3 . . . . 1 1 . . 1 2  10 1 155 70 1 1
55  . . . . . .  10 10 .  03  3 3 . . . . . . . . . . 18  . . . . . 1 1
56  . . 1 23 . .  06 06 .  01  4 4 0 0 0 0 1 1 1 . . 1 2  12  . . . . . 1 .
57  . . . . . 2  . . . . .  02  6 4 0 0 0 0 1 . . . 0 1 . 08  . . . . . 1 .
58  . . 1 22 . 6  . . . . .  .   . . . . . . . . . . . 1 2  18 1 . . . . . 1
59  2 2 1 17 . 5  02 02 4  00  8 7 1 . . 1 . 1 . 1 2  15 1 . . 23 1 .
60  . . 0 00 . 6  . . . . .  .  5 5 1 1 1 1 1 1 1 1 8 1 2  12  . . . . . 1
61  . . 1 13 . 5  . . . .  01  4 2 0 0 0 0 . . . . . 1 2 . . . . . 1 1
62  . 2 1 15 . 3  . . . . .  .  2 4 0 0 0 0 1 . . . 6 . . . . . 155 97 1 1
63  1 1 . . . 2  02 02 .  03  3 3 1 0 0 0 1 0 0 0 0 . . . . . . . 00 0 .
64  . . 1 27 1 8  . . . 2  00  6 5 . . . 1 . . . 1 2  10 1 160 . . 1 1
65  . . . . . .  . . . . .  .   . . . 1 . 1 1 1 . . 1 2  20 . 030 00 0 .
66  2 2 . . . 6  . . . . .  02  7 3 . . . 1 1 . . . . . . . . . . 73 1 0
67  . . . . . 4  . . . . .  .   7 8 1 . . 0 1 1 1 1 . . 1 . . . 170 . . 1 1
68  . . 0 00 0 4  . . . .  01  2 5 0 0 0 0 . . . . 1 2 . . 1 . . . . 1 1
69  . . . . . 2  . . . .  00  3 . 1 1 0 0 1 1 1 1 . . 2 . . 1 150 . . 1 1
70  . . 1 20 . 6  . . . . .  .   . . 0 0 . . 1 . 1 . . 1 . 20 . 130 97 1 1
71  . . 1 18 1 6  . . . .  09  4 3 . . 0 0 1 1 . . 0 1 2 . . 1 . . . 70 1 1
72  . . 1 17 . 4  . . . .  01  5 7 0 0 0 0 . . . . 0 1 2  03  . . . . . . .
73  . . 1 13 1 .  . . . . .  00  1 1 . . . . . . . . . 1 2 . . . . . . . 1
74  . . . . 0 6  06 06 5  01  5 4 1 . . 0 1 . 1 . 8 1 2 . . . 175 . . 1 .
75  . . . . . 6  . . . .  01  4 6 . . 0 0 1 1 1 . . . 1 173 61 1 1
76  . . . . . 5  . . . .  06  6 4 . . . 0 1 1 1 1 8 1 . . . 1 . . . . 1 1
77  . . 1 13 1 5  . . . .  00  5 4 . . 0 0 1 1 . . 0 1 . 20 1 . . . . 1 1
78  . . . . . 4  . . . .  07  5 5 0 0 0 0 . . 1 1 4 1 2  20  . 040 . . . .
```

Society	Variable				
	53-59	60-61	62-64	65-70	71-72
01	11 8 1 0 0 . .	138 ...	... ...	0 7	... ...
02	06 8 0 0 0 0 2	044 ...	456 682 ...	0 2	456 682
03	04 4 1 1 0 . 2	075 ...	120 120 120	1 0 0 . 1 .	120 120
04	07 . . . . 4 2	027 ...	032 032 ...	 7	032 032
05	10 8 . 0 1 4 .	113 225	456 456 ...	1 . 1 0 1 2	456 456
06	. . . 0 0 . . .	063 200	... ...	1 0 0 1 1 .	... ...
07	02 . 0 0 . . .	075 ...	... ...	0	... ...
08	00 0 0 0 . . .	107 069	548 682 ...	1 . 0 0 1 3	548 682
09	08 8 1	032 ...	030 030 ...	. . . . . .	030 030
10	04 0 0 0 . . .	... ...	090 ... 420	1	090 ...
11	06 8 0 3 1 4 0	050 ...	319 319 ...	1 0 1 0 1 .	319 319
12	08 8 1 0 1 4 .	045 ...	... ...	 2	... ...
13	05 0 1 1 . . 1	... ...	... ...	0	... ...
14	04 8 0 0 . 2 .	075 075	... 318 ...	1 1 0 . 1 .	... 318
15	00 . 0 0 . . .	045 ...	030 030 030	 5	030 030
16	. . 0 0 0 . . .	088 ...	... ...	 6	... ...
17	08 0 0 0 . . .	069 ...	... ...	1 0 0 0 . 1	... ...
18	00 6 0 0 . 2 1	050 039	023 023 023	1 . 0 0 1 5	023 023
19	04 . 0 0 . 2 .	113 ...	... ...	1 . . . 1 .	... ...
20	02 . . 0 . . .	325 028	... ...	. 1 . 0 . .	... ...
21	06 0 0	045 ...	... ...	0 2	... ...
22	00 . 0 0 . . 2	075 050	365 365 495	1 . . 0 0 .	365 365
23	00 8 0 0 1 4 .	058 069	013 130 ...	1 0 0 0 0 .	013 130
24	04 0 0 0 . . .	055 ...	... ...	. . . . . .	... ...
25	08 2 1 . . . 1	075 ...	... ...	1	... ...
26	02 6 0 0 1 4 .	075 999	365 365 ...	1 0 0 1 0 .	365 365
27	02 . 0 0 . 4 2	... ...	028 028 ...	1 . 0 0 . .	028 028
28	00 0 . 0 . 4 2	113 ...	191 191 ...	1 . 0 1 0 .	191 191
29	02 0 0 0 . . .	150 013	... ...	1 1 . 0 . .	... ...
30	00 . 0 0 . . 2	088 028	... ...	1 1 0 0 . .	... ...
31	06 . . 0 . 4 1	... ...	... 269 ...	 7	... 269
32	02 . . 0 . 0 .	058 035	053	1 1 . 0 . .	053 ...
33	02 . . 0 . 0 .	032 ...	... 010 ...	0	... 010
34	06 0 1 0 . . 2	... ...	... 432 ...	1 0 . 0 . .	... 432
35	. . . . 0 . 4 .	039 047	002 045 ...	1 0 0 0 0 .	002 045
36	10 6 1 0 1 . .	042 ...	365 365 ...	1	365 365
37	00 . 0 0 . . .	065 ...	... 730 999	1	... 730
38	04 0 1	018 ...	... ...	. . . . . .	... ...
39	06 2 0 0 . 4 2	063 051	365 365 365	1 1 . . 1 .	365 365

Society	53-59	60-61	62-64	65-70	71-72
40	04 . 0 . . .	125 065	... ...	1 0 0 0 . .	... ...
41	. . 0 1 0 . . 1	058 ...	... 500 ...	. . . .	... 500
42	00 . 0 0 . . 1	088 ...	... ...	0 7	... ...
43	06 8 0 . 1 0 .	032 ...	... 365 015	. . . .	... 365
44	02 0 . 0 . 2 2	153 ...	... 282 ...	1 0 0 . . .	... 282
45	07 8 1 1 . . .	069 ...	... ...	0	... ...
46	. . 0 . 0 . 4 .	175 175	003 005 ...	1 1 0 0 . .	003 005
47	06 . . 0 . . .	088 088	365 365 ...	1 0 0 1 1 .	365 365
48	05 8 . . 1 . 2	175 200	... 365 ...	1 0 . . 0 1	... 365
49	08 0	052 039	... ...	1 . 0 1 . 2	
50	08 . 0 0 . 0 2	069 107	... 516 ...	1 1 0 1 1 .	... 516
51	02 . 0 0 . . 2	138 ...	... ...	0	... ...
52	07 . 0	... ...	523 913 ...	 4	523 913
53	06 0 0 0 . 4 2	150 ...	... ...	1 1 0 0 1 .	... ...
54	07 . 1 . 1 . 2	075 138	365 365 ...	1 0 . 0 1 3	365 365
55	08 4 . . 0 . .	... ...	822 457 001	. . . . . .	822 451
56	00 . 0 0 . . 2	082 ...	... ...		... ...
57	. . 0 . . . 0 .	088 125	183 183 183	1 . 0 1 . .	183 183
58	08 . 1 1 . . 2	... ...	... ...	1	... ...
59	. . . . 0 . 3 2	150 225	... 015 015	1 1 1 . 0 .	... 015
60	08 . 0 0 . . 0	039 ...	002 002 ...	0 7	002 002
61	06 2	175 225	... ...	1 . . 0 1 .	... ...
62	08 . 1 1 . 0 .	008 005	092 092 ...	1 0 0 1 0 .	092 092
63	02 0 0 0 . 4 .	200 133	030 130 ...	1 1 0 0 0 .	030 130
64	07 0 1 0 . 4 .	094 090	... 365 ...	1 1 0 0 1 .	... 365
65	00 0 0 0 . . .	017 ...	 084	0	... ...
66	04 8 . 0 1 . .	125 125	281 281 ...	1 1 0 . . .	128 128
67	00 0 0 0 . 4 .	125 175	... 444 ...	1 1 . . 1 .	... 444
68	06 7 0 0 . 0 .	054 ...	038 038 038	. . . . . .	038 038
69	02 . 0 0 . 2 1	100 ...	365 365 ...	 5	365 365
70	07	... ...	... 308 135	1	... 308
71	06 4 0 0 1 . 2	120 ...	029 029 ...	0 5	029 029
72	04 . 0 0 . . 2	063 022	... ...	1 1 0 0 . .	... ...
73	00 . 1 1 . . .	008 ...	... ...	0	... ...
74	04 8 1 1 1 4 .	052 039	... 457 ...	1 . 0 1 1 5	... 457
75	08 8 1 . 1 1 .	032 ...	281 999 018	0	281 999
76	04 . . 0 . 0 .	035 550	224 432 148	1 1 1 0 1 .	224 432
77	04 4 0 0 1 0 .	... ...	185 365 185	0 5	185 365
78	02 0 0 0 . . .	055 ...	112	 3	112 ...

Society   *Variable*

Society   *Variable*

```
Society        Variable
            73-83              84-87

01   0 0 0 0 1 . . . . . .     00 0 . . . .
02   1 0 0 0 1 . . . . . .     15 . . 165
03   0 0 0 . 0 0 . 1 . 0 .     00 0 . . . .
04   0 0 0 0 0 . . . . . .     00 0 . . . .
05   1 1 1 1 1 1 . 1 1 1 0     20 0 . . . .
06   . . . . . 1 1 . . . 1     00 4 . 160
07   1 1 . . . . . . . . .     00 3 . 172
08   1 0 0 0 1 1 0 0 0 . .     80 0 4 . . .
09   . 1 1 . . . . . . . .     00 0 . . . .
10   1 . . . . . . . . . .     00 . 6 167
11   . . . . . 1 . . . . 1     05 1 . 147
12   . . . 0 . . . . . . .     00 4 . 160
13   0 0 0 . . . . . . . .     00 0 0 125
14   0 0 0 . . 0 1 1 1 1 .     00 0 0 . . .
15   . . 1 0 . . . . . . .     00 0 0 130
16   0 . 1 0 0 . . . . . .     40 0 8 133
17   . 1 1 0 0 . . . . . .     00 4 . . . .
18   0 0 . 0 1 1 1 1 . 1 0     15 0 . . . .
19   0 0 0 . 1 1 . . . . .     00 4 . 203
20   1 . . . 0 . . . . . .     70 . . 142
21   0 0 0 . . . . . . . .     00 . . 115
22   . 1 . . 1 1 . 1 . 1 .     60 0 8 160
23   1 . 0 0 0 1 . . 0 . 0     00 1 . 158
24   . . . . . . . . . . .     00 0 . 150
25   0 0 0 . . 1 0 1 . . 0     00 2 2 . . .
26   1 . 0 . 0 1 1 1 . 0 1     02 4 . . . .
27   . . . . . 1 . 1 . 1 0     00 4 . 145
28   . . 0 . . 1 . 0 . . .     00 0 . . . .
29   . 0 0 0 1 1 0 . 0 0 0     00 0 . . . .
30   1 0 0 . 0 1 0 0 . 0 0     00 3 6 162
31   . . . . . . . . . . .     00 2 . 082
32   0 0 0 . 0 1 0 0 . 0 0     30 0 . 138
33   1 . . . . . . . . . .     00 . 8 130
34   0 . . . . . . . . . .     40 2 . 180
35   . . . . . . . . . . .     00 2 . . . .
36   0 . . . . 0 . . . . .     00 0 . 160
37   1 . . . . 1 . 0 . 1 .     00 . . 185
38   . . . . . . . . . . .     70 . 6 253
39   1 0 0 . 1 . . . . . .     10 3 . 178
```

Society	Variable 73-83	84-87
40	1 . . . 1 1 . . . 1 1	00 0 . 135
41	. . . .	00 0 . ...
42	1 0 0	60 0 7 178
43	0	00 . . ...
44	. . 1	00 2 2 ...
45	. . . .	00 . . ...
46	. . . .	00 2 2 ...
47	1 . 1	00 0 . ...
48	1 . . . 1 1 . 1 0 1 0	10 . . 120
49	1 . 1 . . 1 . 1 . . .	00 3 . ...
50	1 0 0 . 0 1 1 1 . 1 .	00 0 . ...
51	1 1 . 0 0	00 4 . 173
52	. . 0 . 0	00 0 . 155
53	0 0 0 0 0 1 . 1 0 0 1	00 0 . ...
54	. . . . . 1	45 0 . 133
55	0 0 0 . 0	00 0 . 205
56	1 . . . 1	10 0 . ...
57	1 0 0 0 1 1 0 0 . 1 .	30 2 . 160
58	1 1 . . . 1	00 0 . 155
59	0 . . . 0 1 1	00 2 . ...
60	. . . .	00 0 . 090
61	1 . 1 . . 1 . . . 1	00 . 6 ...
62	0 0 0 0 0	10 0 . ...
63	1	00 . . 105
64	1 . 1 . 1 1 . 1 1 1 0	10 0 . ...
65	. . . .	30 0 6 ...
66	0 . 1 . 0 . . 1 . . .	00 1 6 155
67	. . . . . 1 . 1 1 . 1	02 4 . ...
68	0 0 0 0 0	30 . . ...
69	1 0 0	45 0 8 230
70	1 1 1 . 1 . . . . 1 .	00 0 . ...
71	1 0 0 . 0	00 4 . ...
72	1 1 1 . . 1	30 . . ...
73	0 0 0 . 0	00 . 3 ...
74	. . . .	00 0 . 103
75	1 . . . 1	40 . . 170
76	. . . . 1 1 1 . . 1	00 . . 158
77	0 0 0 . 0	00 0 2 ...
78	. . . .	80 0 . 165

Notes for Appendix

[1] Arithmetic means given for six correlations and six numbers of cases for the correlations.

[2] For some cases in the sample, Friendly (1956) has attempted ratings of some variables similar to variables we have rated. The Friendly ratings were given to us by Professor John W. M. Whiting. For the variable of degree of ghost fear (variable 25 in our tabulations), the Friendly sample and ours have seven cases in common and correlate only -.03; however, in all seven cases, the two rating sets agree on presence of ghost fear (variable 24 in our tabulations). On frequency of actual self-injury (variable 6 in our tabulations) the two sets of ratings have been made on nine common cases and correlate .89. On presence of name taboo (variable 54 in our tabulations), the two samples overlap in twelve cases; they correlate only .22 on extent of name taboo and agree on presence or absence of name taboo in only seven of the twelve cases. The Friendly ratings provide strong convergent validity for presence of ghost fear and frequency of self-mutilation, but not for degree of ghost fear or extent of name taboo. However, the rating instructions and procedures and the sources used may be so discrepant between the Friendly study and ours that the comparison of ratings is at best only suggestive of possible convergent validity or of validity problems.

References

Part 1.

Sources of the Ethnographic Extracts

01 Abipone—Dobrizhoffer (1822)

02 Ainu—Batchelor (1892, 1927); Sugiura and Befu (1962)

03 Andamanese—Radcliffe-Brown (1964)

04 Aweikoma—Henry (1941)

05 Azande—Gero (1968)

06 Balinese—Covarrubias (1937); Geertz (1964, 1966)

07 Thai villagers—deYoung (1955); Young (1907)

08 Basque—Douglass (1969)

09 Carib—Gillin (1936)

10 Chinese villagers—Fei (1939); Fei and Chang (1945)

11 Chippewa—Densmore (1913, 1929); Hilger (1951)

12 Comanche—Hoebel (1939, 1940); Wallace and Hoebel (1952)

13 Copper Eskimo—Jenness (1922)

14 Cubeo—Goldman (1948, 1963)

15 Eastern Timbira—Nimuendajú (1946)

16 Egyptian Fellahin—Ammār (1954); Blackman (1927); Klunzinger (1878)

17 Eyak—Birket-Smith and De Laguna (1938)

18 Ganda—Mair (1933, 1934, 1940); Roscoe (1911)

19 Garo—Burling (1963)

20 Gheg—Coon (1950); Durham (1928)

21 Gros Ventre—Flannery (1953); Kroeber (1908)

22 Haitians—Herskovits (1937)

23 Hausa—Barkow (1970); Greenberg (1946); Smith (1955, 1965); Tremearne (1914)

24 Hidatsa—Bowers (1965); Lowie (1917); Matthews (1877)

25 Hill Maria Gond—Grigson (1938)

26 Huron—Tooker (1964)

27 Ibo—Basden (1966a, 1966b)

28 Ifugao—Barton (1946, 1969)

29 Japanese—Beardsley, Hall, and Ward (1959); Embree (1939)

30 Javanese—C. Geertz (1960); H. Geertz (1961); Koentjaraningrat (1960)

31 Jivaro—Karsten (1935); Stirling (1938)

32 Kafa—Bieber (1923); Huntingford (1955)

33 Kapauku—Pospisil (1958, 1963)

34 Kaska—Honigmann (1949, 1954)

35 Katab—Meek (1931)

36 Klamath—Spier (1930); Voegelin (1942)

37 Koreans—Osgood (1951)

38 Lapps—Collinder (1949); Indiana University (1955); Itkonen (1948); Karsten (1955); Nordström (1930); Pehrson (1957); Vorren and Manker (1962); Whitaker (1955)

39 Lepcha—Das and Banerjee (1962); Gorer (1967); Morris (1938)

40 Lolo—Lin (1961)

41 Manus—Fortune (1935); Mead (1930a, 1933)

42 Marshallese—Erdland (1914); Mason (1954); Spoehr (1949)

43 Masai—Hollis (1905, 1910); Leakey (1930)

44 Mbundu—Childs (1949); Hambly (1934); McCulloch (1952)

45 Mbuti—Schebesta (1933); Turnbull (1961, 1965a, 1965b)

46 Mende—Little (1951)

47 Micmac—Denys (1908); Le Clercq (1910)

48 Miskito—Conzemius (1932)

49 Murngin—Warner (1958)

50 Nicobarese—Man (1932)

51 Burmese villagers—Nash (1965); Scott (1882)

52 Omaha—J. O. Dorsey (1884); Fletcher and LaFlesche (1911)

53 Orokaiva—Williams (1930)

54 Papago—Joseph, Spicer, and Chesky (1949); Underhill (1936, 1939, 1940, 1946)

55 Pawnee—G. A. Dorsey (1904); G. A. Dorsey and Murie (1940)

56 Samoans—Ablon (1970); Mead (1930b); Stair (1897); Turner (1861, 1884)

57 Santal—Culshaw (1949)

58 Semang—Evans (1937)

59 Seniang—Deacon (1934)

60 Shavante—Maybury-Lewis (1967)

61 Shilluk—Seligman and Seligman (1932); Westermann (1912)

62 Siriono—Holmberg (1950)

63 Siwans—'Abd Allah (1917); Belgrave (1923); Cline (1936)

64 Thonga—Junod (1927)

65 Tikopia—Firth (1936, 1967)

66 Toda—Rivers (1967)

67 Trobrianders—Malinowski (1922, 1935, 1948, 1969)

68 Trukese—Gladwin and Sarason (1953); Goodenough (1951)

69 Tswana—Schapera (1938, 1940, 1950, 1953)

70 Tupinamba—Abbeville (1614); Anchieta (1846); Cardim (1906); Evereux (1864); Souza (1851); Thevet (1878, 1928)

71 Twana—Elmendorf (1960)

72 Vanua Levu Fijians—Quain (1948)

73 Vedda—Bailey (1863); Seligman and Seligman (1911)

74 Walbiri—Meggitt (1965)

75 Western Apache—Goodwin (1935, 1942)

76 Wukchumni—Gayton (1948)

77 Yurok—Elmendorf (1960); Kroeber (1925, 1960)

78 Zapotec—Parsons (1936)

Part 2.

Works Cited

Abbeville, Claude d', Father

    1614   *Histoire de la mission des Pères Capucins en l'Isle de Maragnan et terres circonvoisines,* Paris, Huby.

'Abd Allah, M. M.

    1917   "Siwan customs," *Harvard African Studies 1*: 1-28.

Ablon, Joan

    1970   "The Samoan funeral in urban America," *Ethnology 9*: 209-27.

Ahern, Emily M.

    1973   *The cult of the dead in a Chinese village,* Stanford, Stanford University Press.

'Ammār, Hāmid

    1954   *Growing up in an Egyptian village; Silwa, province of Aswan,* London, Routledge and Paul.

Anchieta, José de

    1846   "Informação dos casamentos dos Indios do Brasil," 2d ed., *Instituto Histórico e Geográphico dó Brasil, Revista Trimensal de Historia et Geographia 8*: 254-62.

Avebury, John Lubbock, Baron

    1902   *The origin of civilisation and the primitive condition of man,* 6th ed., London, Longmans, Green.

Averill, James R.

    1968   "Grief: its nature and significance," *Psychological Bulletin* 70: 721-48.

Bach, George R., and Peter Wyden

    1968   *The intimate enemy*, New York, Avon.

Bailey, John

    1863   "An account of the wild tribes of the Veddahs of Ceylon," *Ethnological Society of London, Transactions* 2: 278-320.

Bakan, D.

    1966   "The test of significance in psychological research," *Psychological Bulletin 66*: 423-37.

Barkow, Jerome H.

    1970   *Hausa and Maguzawa: processes of group differentiation in a rural area in North Central State, Nigeria*, unpublished doctoral dissertation, University of Chicago.

Baroja, Pío

    1962   *The restlessness of Shanti Andia and selected stories* (translated by A. Kerrigan and E. Kerrigan), New York, Signet.

Barton, Roy Franklin

    1946   "The religion of the Ifugaos," *American Anthropological Association, Memoir 65*.

    1969   *Ifugao law*, Berkeley, University of California Press (originally published in 1919).

Basden, George Thomas

    1966a   *Among the Ibos of Nigeria*, London, Cass (originally published in 1921).

    1966b   *Niger Ibos*, London, Cass (originally published in 1938).

Batchelor, John

    1892   *The Ainu of Japan*, New York, F. H. Revell Co.

    1927   *Ainu life and lore*, Tokyo, Kyobunkwan.

Beardsley, Richard K., John W. Hall. and Robert E. Ward

1959   *Village Japan*, Chicago, University of Chicago Press.

Becker, H.

1933   "The sorrow of bereavement," *Journal of Abnormal and Social Psychology 27*: 391-410.

Belgrave, C. Dalrymple

1923   *Siwa, the oasis of Jupiter Ammon*, London, John Lane, the Bodley Head.

Bem, D. J.

1972   "Self-perception theory," in Leonard Berkowitz, ed., *Advances in Experimental Social Psychology, vol. 6*, New York, Academic Press: 1-62.

Bendann, Effie

1930   *Death customs*, London, Kegan Paul, Trench & Trubner.

Benedict, Ruth F.

1938   "Continuities and discontinuities in cultural conditioning," *Psychiatry 1*: 161-67.

Berardo, F.

1970   "Survivorship and social isolation: the case of the aged widower," *Family Coordinator 19*: 11-25.

Berkowitz, Leonard

1962   *Aggression: a social psychological analysis*, New York, McGraw-Hill.

Bieber, Friedrich J.

1923   *Kaffa, ein altkuschitisches Volkstum in Inner-Afrika, bd. 2*, Vienna, Verlag der Anthropos.

Bindra, D.

1972   "Weeping: a problem of many facets," *British Psychological Society, Bulletin 25*: 281-84.

Birket-Smith, Kaj, and Frederica De Laguna

1938   *The Eyak Indians of the Copper River Delta, Alaska*, København, Levin & Munksgaard.

Blackman, Winifred S.

1927   The Fellahin of Upper Egypt, London, Harrap.

Blauner, R.

1966   "Death and social structure," Psychiatry 29: 378-94.

Bloch, Maurice

1971   Placing the dead: tombs, ancestral villages and kinship organization in Madagascar, New York, Seminar Press.

Bowers, Alfred W.

1965   "Hidatsa social and ceremonial organization," U.S. Bureau of American Ethnology, Bulletin 194.

Bowlby, J.

1961   "Process of mourning," International Journal of Psycho-Analysis 42: 317-40.

Bowman, LeRoy E.

1959   The American funeral; a study of guilt, extravagance, and sublimity, Washington, D.C., Public Affairs Press.

Brandt, Vincent S. R.

1971   A Korean village between farm and sea, Cambridge, Harvard University Press.

Brehm, Jack W., and Arthur R. Cohen

1962   Explorations in cognitive dissonance, New York, Wiley.

Burling, Robbins

1963   Rengsanggri; family and kinship in a Garo village, Philadelphia, University of Pennsylvania Press.

Campbell, Donald T.

1961   "The mutual methodological relevance of anthropology and psychology," in Francis L. K. Hsu, ed., Psychological Anthropology, Homewood, Ill., Dorsey Press: 333-52.

Campbell, Donald T., and Donald W. Fiske

1959   "Convergent and discriminant validation by the multi-trait-multimethod matrix," Psychological Bulletin 56: 81-105.

Cardim, Fernão

1906   "A treatise of Brasil *and* articles touching the dutie of the Kings Majestie our Lord, and to the common good of all the estate of Brasill. Edited by Samuel Purchas," *Hakluytus Posthumus or Purchas His Pilgrimes, vol. 16*, Glasgow, MacLehose: 417-517.

Carter, Hugh, Paul C. Glick, and Sarah Lewit

1955   "Some demographic characteristics of recently married persons: comparisons of registration data and sample survey data," *American Sociological Review 20*: 165-72.

Carter, William E.

1968   "Secular reinforcement in Aymara death ritual," *American Anthropologist 70*: 238-63.

Childs, Gladwyn Murray

1949   *Umbundu kinship and character*, London, published for the International African Institute and the Witwatersrand and University Press by Oxford University Press.

Clayton, Paula J.

1975   "The effect of living alone on bereavement symptoms," *American Journal of Psychiatry 132*: 133-37.

Clayton, Paula J., Lynn Desmarais and George Winokur

1968   "A study of normal bereavement," *American Journal of Psychiatry 125*: 168-78.

Cline, Walter B.

1936   "Notes on the people of Siwah and El Garah in the Libyan desert," *General Series in Anthropology 4*, Menasha, Wis., Banta.

Cohen, Ronald

1967   *The Kanuri of Bornu*, New York, Holt, Rinehart and Winston.

Collinder, Björn

1949   *The Lapps*, Princeton, Princeton University Press for the American Scandinavian Foundation.

Conzemius, Eduard

    1932   "Ethnographic survey of the Miskito and Sumu Indians of Honduras and Nicaragua," *U.S. Bureau of American Ethnology, Bulletin 106.*

Coon, Carleton S.

    1950   "The mountains of giants: a racial and cultural study of the North Albanian Mountain Ghegs," *Harvard University, Peabody Museum of American Archaeology and Ethnology, Papers 23, no. 3*: 1-105.

Coppinger, Robert M., and Paul C. Rosenblatt

    1968   "Romantic love and subsistence dependence of spouses," *Southwestern Journal of Anthropology 24*: 310-19.

Covarrubias, Miguel

    1937   *Island of Bali,* New York, A. A. Knopf.

Culshaw, W. J.

    1949   *Tribal heritage: a study of the Santals,* London, Lutterworth Press.

Das, Amal Kumar, and Swapan Kumar Banerjee

    1962   *The Lepchas of Darjeeling District,* Calcutta, Tribal Welfare Department, Government of West Bengal.

Deacon, Arthur B.

    1934   *Malekula, a vanishing people in the New Hebrides,* London, G. Routledge and Sons.

Densmore, Frances

    1913   "Chippewa music, Part II," *U.S. Bureau of American Ethnology, Bulletin 53.*

    1929   "Chippewa customs," *U.S. Bureau of American Ethnology, Bulletin 86.*

Denys, Nicolas

    1908   "The description and natural history of the coasts of North America (Arcadia)," in W. F. Ganong, ed., *Publications of the Champlain Society, vol. 2,* Toronto: 399-452.

deYoung, John E.

1955   *Village life in modern Thailand*, Berkeley, University of California Press.

Dobrizhoffer, Martin

1822   *An account of the Abipones, vol. 2*, London, Murray.

Dollard, John, Leonard W. Doob, Neal E. Miller, O. H. Mowrer, and Robert R. Sears

1939   *Frustration and aggression*, New Haven, published for the Institute of Human Relations by Yale University Press.

Donaldson, P. J.

1972   "Denying death: a note regarding some ambiguities in the current discussion," *Omega 3*: 285-90.

Dorsey, George A.

1904   *Traditions of the Skidi Pawnee*, London, D. Nutt.

Dorsey, George A., and James R. Murie

1940   "Notes on Skidi Pawnee society," *Field Museum of Natural History, Anthropological Series 27*: 67-119.

Dorsey, James Owen

1884   "Omaha sociology," *U.S. Bureau of Ethnology, Annual Report 3*: 205-370.

Douglass, William A.

1969   *Death in Murelaga*, Seattle, University of Washington Press.

Driver, Harold E., and Richard P. Chaney

1970   "Cross-cultural sampling and Galton's problem," in Raoul Naroll and Ronald Cohen, eds., *Handbook of Method in Cultural Anthropology*, Garden City, N.Y., Natural History Press: 990-1003 (reissued 1973 by Columbia University Press).

Dumont, Richard G., and Dennis C. Foss

1972   *The American view of death: acceptance or denial?* Cambridge, Mass., Schenkman.

Dunn, O. J., and V. Clark

1969   "Correlation coefficients measured on the same individuals," *Journal of the American Statistical Association* *64*: 366-77.

Durkheim, Émile

1915   *The elementary forms of religious life*, New York, Macmillan.

Durham, Mary Edith

1928   *Some tribal origins, laws and customs of the Balkans*, London, George Allen and Unwin.

Edgington, E. S.

1966   "Statistical inference and nonrandom samples," *Psychological Bulletin 66*: 485-87.

Eliot, T. D.

1955   "Bereavement: inevitable but not insurmountable," in Howard P. Becker and Reuben Hill, eds., *Family, Marriage and Parenthood*, Boston, Heath: chap. 22.

Elmendorf, William W.

1960   "The structure of Twana culture, with comparative notes on the structure of Yurok culture by Alfred L. Kroeber," *Washington State University Research Studies, Monographic Supplement 2*.

Embree, John F.

1939   *Suye Mura*, Chicago, University of Chicago Press.

Erdland, P. August

1914   "Die Marshall-Insulaner, Leben und Sitte, Sinn und Religion eines Südsee-Volkes," *Anthropos-Bibliothek, II, 1, Ethnological Monographs*, Münster i. W., Aschendorff.

Estes, William K.

1959   "The statistical approach to learning theory," in Sigmund Koch, ed., *Psychology: A Study of a Science, vol. 2, General Systematic Formulations, Learning, and Special Processes*, New York, McGraw-Hill: 380-491.

Evans, Ivor H. N.

1937   *The Negritos of Malaya*, Cambridge, University Press.

Evereux, Yves d'

1864   *Voyage dans le nord du Brésil fait durant les années 1613 et 1614*, Paris and Leipzig, A. Franck.

Faron, Louis C.

1963   "Death and fertility rites of the Mapuche (Araucanian) Indians of central Chile," *Ethnology 2*: 135-56.

Fei Hsiao-tung

1939   *Peasant life in China: a field study of country life in the Yangtze Valley*, London, G. Routledge and Sons.

Fei Hsiao-tung, and Chang Chih-i

1945   *Earthbound China: a study of rural economy in Yunnan*, Chicago, University of Chicago Press.

Ferster, C. B.

1973   "A functional analysis of depression," *American Psychologist 28*: 857-70.

Festinger, Leon

1957   *A theory of cognitive dissonance*, Evanston, Row, Peterson.

Firth, Raymond

1936   *We, the Tikopia*, London, Allen and Unwin.

1967   *Tikopia ritual and belief*, Boston, Beacon Press.

Flannery, Regina

1953   "The Gros Ventres of Montana: Part 1, social life," *Catholic University of America, Anthropological Series 15*.

Fletcher, Alice C., and Francis LaFlesche

1911   "The Omaha tribe," *U.S. Bureau of American Ethnology, Annual Report 27*: 15-672.

Forde, C. Daryll

    1962   "Death and succession: an analysis of Yakö mortuary ritual," in Max Gluckman, ed., *Essays on the Ritual of Social Relations*, Manchester, Manchester Unversity Press: 89-123.

Fortune, Reo F.

    1935   *Manus religion*, Philadelphia, American Philosophical Society.

Frazer, James G.

    1933-   *The fear of the dead in primitive religion* (3 vols.),
     36   London, Macmillan.

Freud, Sigmund

    1953   *A general introduction to psychoanalysis* (translated by J. Riviere), New York, Permabooks (originally published in 1920).

    1959   "Mourning and melancholia," *Collected papers of . . . (vol. 4), Papers on Metapsychology, Papers on Applied Psychoanalysis*, New York, Basic Books: 152-70 (originally published in 1917).

Fried, Morton H.

    1963   "Grieving for a lost home," in Leonard J. Duhl, ed., *The Urban Condition*, New York, Basic Books: 151-71.

Friendly, Joan P.

    1956   *A cross-cultural study of ascetic mourning behavior*, unpublished honors thesis, Cambridge. Mass., Radcliffe College, Department of Social Relations.

Fulton, Robert L.

    1961   "The clergyman and the funeral director: a study in role conflict," *Social Forces 39*: 317-23.

Gayton, Anna H.

    1948   "Yokuts and Western Mono ethnography," *Anthropological Records 10*.

Geertz, Clifford

    1960   *The religion of Java*, New York, The Free Press of Glencoe.

1964 "Tihingan: a Balinese village," *Bijdragen tot de Taal-, Land- en Volkenkunde 120*: 1-33.

1966 "Person, time and conduct in Bali: an essay in cultural analysis," *Yale University, Southeast Asia Studies, Cultural Report Series 14*: 1-85.

Geertz, Hildred

1961 *The Javanese family*, New York, The Free Press of Glencoe.

Gennep, Arnold van

1960 *The rites of passage* (translated by Monika B. Vizedom and Gabrielle L. Caffee), Chicago, University of Chicago Press (originally published in 1909).

Gero, F.

1968 *Death among the Azande of the Sudan* by F. Giorgetti, (translated by W. H. Paxman), Museum Combonianum 22, Bologna, Editrice Nigrizia.

Gillin, John P.

1936 "The Barama River Carib of British Guiana," *Harvard University, Peabody Museum of American Archaeology and Ethnology, Papers 14*: 1-274.

Gladwin, Thomas, and Seymour B. Sarason

1953 "Truk: man in paradise," *Viking Fund Publications in Anthropology 20*.

Glick, I. O., R. S. Weiss, and C. M. Parkes

1974 *The first year of bereavement*, New York, Wiley-Interscience.

Goldman, Irving

1948 "Tribes of the Uaupes-Caqueta Region," *U.S. Bureau of American Ethnology, Bulletin 143, vol. 3*: 763-98.

1963 *The Cubeo Indians of the Northwest Amazon*, Urbana, University of Illinois Press.

Goldschmidt, Walter

1973 "Guilt and pollution in Sebei mortuary rituals," *Ethos 1*: 75-105.

Goodenough, Ward H.

1951   "Property, kin and community on Truk," *Yale University Publications in Anthropology 46.*

Goodwin, Grenville

1935   "The social divisions and economic life of the Western Apache," *American Anthropologist, n.s. 37:* 55-64.

1942   *The social organization of the Western Apache,* Chicago, University of Chicago Press.

Goody, Jack

1962   *Death, property and the ancestors,* Stanford, Stanford University Press.

Gorer, Geoffrey

1965   *Death, grief, and mourning,* New York, Doubleday.

1967   *Himalayan village,* 2d ed., New York, Basic Books.

1973   "Death, grief, and mourning in Britain," in E. J. Anthony and C. Koupernik, eds., *The child in his family: the impact of disease and death,* New York, Wiley: 423-38.

Greenacre, P.

1966   "Summary of discussion remarks on Dr. Löfgren's paper," *International Journal of Psycho-Analysis 47:* 381-83.

Greenberg, Joseph H.

1946   "The influence of Islam on a Sudanese religion," *American Ethnological Society, Monograph 10,* Seattle, University of Washington Press.

Grigson, Wilfrid Vernon

1938   *The Maria Gonds of Bastar,* London, Oxford University Press.

Gulliver, Philip H.

1964   "The Arusha family," in Robert F. Gray and Philip H. Gulliver, eds., *The Family Estate in Africa,* Boston, Boston University Press: 197-229.

Habenstein, Robert W.

1968   "The social organization of death," *International Encyclopedia of the Social Sciences, vol. 4*, New York, Macmillan: 26-28.

Hambly, Wilfrid D.

1934   "The Ovimbundu of Angola," Chicago, *Field Museum of Natural History, Anthropological Series 21, no. 2*: 87-362 + 83 plates.

Heimlich, H. J., and A. H. Kutscher

1970   "The family's reaction to terminal illness," in B. Schoenberg, A. C. Carr, D. Peretz, and A. H. Kutscher, eds., *Loss and Grief: Psychological Management in Medical Practice*, New York, Columbia University Press: 270-79.

Henry, Jules

1964   *Jungle people*, New York, Vintage (originally published in 1941 by J. J. Augustin).

Herskovits, Melville J.

1937   *Life in a Haitian valley*, New York, A. A. Knopf.

Hertz, R.

1960   *Death and the right hand* (translated by Rodney Needham and C. Needham), Glencoe, Ill., Free Press.

Hickerson, Harold

1960   "The feast of the dead among the seventeenth century Algonkians of the Upper Great Lakes," *American Anthropologist 62*: 81-107.

Hilger, M. Inez

1951   "Chippewa child life and its cultural background," *U.S. Bureau of American Ethnology, Bulletin 146*.

Hiltz, S. R.

1975   "Helping widows: group discussions as a therapeutic technique," *Family Coordinator 24*: 331-36.

Hobson, C. J.

1964   "Widows at Blackton," *New Society*, 24 September: 13-16.

Hocart, A. M.

1931   "Death customs," *Encyclopedia of the Social Sciences,* *vol. 5,* New York, Macmillan: 21-27.

Hoebel, Edward Adamson

1939   "Comanche and Hekandika Shoshone relationship systems," *American Anthropologist, n.s. 41:* 440-57.

1940   "The political organization and law-ways of the Comanche Indians," *American Anthropological Association Memoir 54.*

Hollis, Alfred C.

1905   *The Masai; their language and folklore,* Oxford, Clarendon Press.

1910   "A note on the Masai system of relationship," *Royal Anthropological Institute of Great Britain and Ireland, Journal 40:* 473-82.

Holmberg, Allan R.

1950   "Nomads of the long bow," *Smithsonian Institution, Institute of Social Anthropology Publications 10,* Washington, D.C., U.S. Government Printing Office.

Honigmann, John J.

1949   "Culture and ethos of Kaska society," *Yale University Publications in Anthropology 40.*

1954   "The Kaska Indians, an ethnographic reconstruction," *Yale University Publications in Anthropology 51* (reissued in 1964 by HRAF Press, New Haven).

Huntingford, G. W. B.

1955   *The Galla of Ethiopia: the kingdoms of Kafa and Janjero,* London, International African Institute.

Indiana, University, Graduate Program of Uralic and Asian Studies

1955   *The Lapps* (by Eeva K. Minn), New Haven, Human Relations Area Files.

Itkonen, Toivo I.

1948   *Suomen Lappalaiset vuoteen 1945,* Helsinki, Söderström.

Jenness, Diamond

    1922   "The life of the Copper Eskimos," *Report of the Canadian Arctic Expedition, 1913-1918, 12*: 5-227.

Jensen, G. D., and J. G. Wallace

    1967   "Family mourning process," *Family Process 6*: 56-66.

Joseph, Alice, Rosamond B. Spicer, and Jane Chesky

    1949   *The desert people: a study of the Papago Indians*, Chicago, University of Chicago Press.

Junod, H. A.

    1927   *The life of a South African tribe*, 2d ed., rev. (2 vols.), London, Macmillan.

Kalish, R. A., and D. K. Reynolds

    1973   "Phenomenological reality and post-death contact," *Journal for the Scientific Study of Religion 12*: 209-21.

Karsten, Rafael

    1935   *The head hunters of Western Amazonas*, Helsinki, Finska Vetenskaps-Societeten.

    1955   *The religion of the Samek: ancient beliefs and cults of the Scandinavian and Finnish Lapps*, Leiden, Brill.

Kastenbaum, R., and R. Aisenberg

    1972   *The psychology of death*, New York, Springer.

Kennell, J. H., H. Slyter, and M. H. Klaus

    1970   "The mourning response of parents to the death of a newborn infant," *New England Journal of Medicine 283*: 344-49.

Kiesler, C. A.

    1971   *The psychology of commitment*, New York, Academic Press.

Klinger, E.

    1975   "Consequence of commitment to and disengagement from incentives," *Psychological Review 82*: 1-25.

Klunzinger, K. B.

1878   *Upper Egypt: its people and its products,* New York, Scribner, Armstrong.

Köbben, André J. F.

1967   "Why exceptions? The logic of cross-cultural analysis," *Current Anthropology 8*: 3-19.

Koentjaraningrat, R. M.

1960   "The Javanese of South Central Java," in George Peter Murdock, ed., *Social Structure in Southeast Asia,* Chicago, Quadrangle Books: 88-115.

Kroeber, Alfred L.

1908   "Ethnology of the Gros Ventre," *American Museum of Natural History, Anthropological Papers 1*: Pt. IV, 145-281.

1925   "The Yurok," *Handbook of the Indians of California, U.S. Bureau of American Ethnology, Bulletin 78*: 1-97.

1960   "Comparative notes on the structure of Yurok culture," in William W. Elmendorf, *The Structure of Twana Culture, Washington State University, Research Studies, Monographic Supplement 2.*

Krupp, G. R., and B. Kligfeld

1962   "The bereavement reaction: a cross-cultural evaluation," *Journal of Religion and Health 1*: 222-46.

Kubler-Ross, E.

1969   *On death and dying,* New York, Macmillan.

1972   "On the use of psychopharmacologic agents for the dying patient and the bereaved," *Journal of Thanatology 2*: 563-66.

Kurtz, D. C., and J. Boardman

1971   *Greek burial customs,* Ithaca, N.Y., Cornell University Press.

Kutscher, A. H.

1970   "Practical aspects of bereavement," in B. Schoenberg, A. C. Carr, D. Peretz, and A. H. Kutscher, eds., *Loss and*

Grief: Psychological Management in Medical Practice,
New York, Columbia University Press: 280-97.

Labovitz, S.

1970 "The nonutility of significance tests: the significance
of tests of significance reconsidered," *Pacific Sociological Review 13*: 141-48.

Lafitau, Joseph François

1724 *Moeurs des sauvages amériquains, comparées aux
moeurs des premiers temps* (2 vols.), Paris, Saugrain
l'aîné (cited in Hertz 1960).

Leakey, L. S. B.

1930 "Some notes on the Masai of Kenya Colony," *Royal
Anthropological Institute of Great Britain and Ireland,
Journal 60*: 185-209.

Le Clercq, Chrestien, Father

1910 "New relation of Gaspesia," in W. F. Ganong, ed.,
Publications of the Champlain Society, vol. 5, Toronto:
61-321.

Lin, Yueh-hua

1961 *The Lolo of Liang Shan,* New Haven, Human Relations
Area Files Press.

Lindemann, Erich

1944 "Symptomatology and management of acute grief,"
American Journal of Psychiatry 101: 141-48.

Little, Kenneth L.

1951 *The Mende of Sierra Leone,* London, Routledge &
Kegan Paul.

Löfgren, L. B.

1966 "On weeping," *International Journal of Psycho-Analysis 47*: 375-81.

Lopata, H. Z.

1973 *Widowhood in an American city,* Cambridge, Mass.,
Schenkman.

Lowie, Robert H.

  1917   "Notes on the social organizations and customs of the
           Mandan, Hidatsa, and Crow Indians," *American Mu-
           seum of Natural History, Anthropological Papers 21*:
           1-99.

Lykken, David T.

  1968   "Statistical significance in psychological research,"
           PsychologicalBulletin 70: 151-59.

Maddison, D.. and B. Raphael

  1972   "Normal bereavement as an illness requiring care:
           psychopharmacological   approaches,"   *Journal   of
           Thanatology 2*: 785-98.

Mair, Lucy Philip

  1933   "Baganda land tenure," *Africa 6*: 187-205.

  1934   *An African people in the twentieth century*, London,
           George Routledge and Sons.

  1940   *Native marriage in Buganda*, London, Oxford Uni-
           versity Press for the International African Institute.

Malinowski, Bronislaw

  1922   *Argonauts of the western Pacific*, London, George
           Routledge and Sons.

  1935   *Coral gardens and their magic* (2 vols.), London, Allen
           and Unwin.

  1948   *Magic, science and religion*, Glencoe, Ill., The Free
           Press.

  1969   *The sexual life of savages in northwestern Melanesia*,
           New York, Harcourt, Brace and World (originally
           published in 1929 by Horace Liveright).

Man, Edward Horace

  1932   *The Nicobar Islands and their people*, Guildford, Eng-
           land, printed and published for the Royal Anthropo-
           logical Institute of Great Britain and Ireland by
           Billing and Sons.

Mandelbaum, David G.

1959   "Social uses of funeral rites," in H. Feifel, ed., *The Meaning of Death*, New York, McGraw-Hill: 189-217.

Mandler, G.

1964   "The interruption of behavior." *Nebraska Symposium on Motivation 12:* 163-219.

Marris, P.

1958   *Widows and their families*, London, Routledge & Kegan Paul.

1974   *Loss and change*, New York, Pantheon.

Mason, Leonard

1954   *Relocation of the Bikini Marshallese: a study in group migration*, unpublished doctoral dissertation, New Haven, Yale University.

Matchett, William Foster

1972   "Repeated hallucinatory experiences as a part of the mourning process among Hopi Indian women," *Psychiatry 35:* 185-94.

Matthews, Washington

1877   "Ethnography and philology of the Hidatsa Indians," *U.S. Geological and Geographic Survey, Miscellaneous Publications 7.*

Maybury-Lewis, David

1967   *Akwē-Shavante society*, Oxford, Clarendon Press.

McCulloch, Merran

1952   "The Ovimbundu of Angola," *Ethnographic Survey of Africa, West Central Africa, Pt. 2*, London, International African Institute.

Mead, Margaret

1930a   *Growing up in New Guinea: a comparative study of primitive education*, New York, Morrow.

1930b "Social organization of Manua," *Bernice P. Bishop Museum, Bulletin 76.*

1933 "Kinship in the Admiralty Islands," *American Museum of Natural History, Anthropological Papers 34*: 181-358.

Meek, Charles K.

1931 *Tribal studies in northern Nigeria* (2 vols.), London, Kegan Paul, Trench, Trubner.

Meggitt, Mervyn J.

1965 *Desert people*, Chicago, University of Chicago Press.

Mitchell, M. E.

1967 *The child's attitude to death*, New York, Schocken.

Mitford, Jessica

1963 *The American way of death*, New York, Simon and Schuster.

Morris, John

1938 *Living with Lepchas*, London, Heinemann.

Moyer, K. E.

1971 "The physiology of aggression and the implications for aggression control," in J. L. Singer, ed., *The Control of Aggression and Violence*, New York, Academic Press: 61-92.

Murdock, George Peter

1949 *Social structure*, New York, Macmillan.

1967 *Ethnographic atlas*, Pittsburgh, University of Pittsburgh Press.

1968 "World sampling provinces," *Ethnology 7*: 305-26.

Murdock, George Peter, et al.

1962- "Ethnographic atlas," *Ethnology 1* to date.

Murdock, George Peter, and Douglas R. White

1969 "Standard cross-cultural sample," *Ethnology 8*: 329-69.

Naroll, Raoul

1961   "Two solutions to Galton's problem," *Philosophy of Science 28*: 15-39.

1962   *Data quality control—a new research technique: prolegomena to a cross-cultural study of culture stress,* New York, Free Press of Glencoe.

Naroll, Raoul, and Ronald Cohen

1970   *A handbook of method in cultural anthropology,* Garden City, N.Y., Natural History Press (reissued 1973 by Columbia University Press).

Naroll, Raoul, and Roy G. D'Andrade

1963   "Two further solutions to Galton's problem," *American Anthropologist 65*: 1053-67.

Nash, Manning

1965   *The golden road to modernity,* New York, Wiley.

Nimuendajú, Curt

1946   "The Eastern Timbira," *University of California Publications in American Archaeology and Ethnology 41.*

Nordström, E. B. E.

1930   *Tent folk of the far north,* London, Jenkins.

Osgood, Cornelius

1951   *The Koreans and their culture,* New York, Ronald Press.

Parkes, Colin Murray

1970   "The first year of bereavement: a longitudinal study of the reactions of London widows to the death of their husbands," *Psychiatry 33*: 444-67.

1972   *Bereavement: studies of grief in adult life,* New York, International Universities Press.

Parsons, Elsie C.

1936   *Mitla: town of souls,* Chicago, University of Chicago Press.

Pehrson, Robert N.

1957 "The bilateral network of social relations in Könkämä Lapp District," *Indiana University Publications, Slavic and East European Series 5*: 1-128.

Perry, R. J.

1972 "Structural resiliency and the danger of the dead: the Western Apache," *Ethnology 11*: 380-85.

Pine, V. R.

1972 "Social organization and death," *Omega 3*: 149-53.

Pospisil, Leopold

1958 "Kapauku Papuäns and their law," *Yale University Publications in Anthropology 54* (reprinted by HRAF Press in 1964).

1963 "Kapauku Papuan economy," *Yale University Publications in Anthropology 67* (reprinted by HRAF Press in 1972).

Quain, Buell H.

1948 *Fijian village*, Chicago, University of Chicago Press.

Radcliffe-Brown, Alfred R.

1964 *The Andaman Islanders*, New York, Free Press of Glencoe (originally published in 1922).

Rees, W. D.

1971 "The hallucinations of widowhood," *British Medical Journal 4*: 37-41.

Rivers, William H. R.

1967 *The Todas*, Osterhout, Netherlands, Anthropological Publications (originally published by Macmillan in 1906).

Romm, M. E.

1970 "Loss of sexual function in the female," in B. Schoenberg, A. C. Carr, D. Peretz, and A. H. Kutscher, eds., *Loss and Grief: Psychological Management in Medical Practice*, New York, Columbia University Press: 178-88.

Roscoe, John

1911 *The Baganda*, London, Macmillan.

Rosenblatt, Paul C.

1974a   *Needed research on commitment in marriage,* paper
         given at the Symposium on Close Social Relations,
         University of Massachusetts, Amherst, May 31, 1974.

1974b   "Cross-cultural perspective on attraction," in T. L.
         Huston, ed., *Foundations of Interpersonal Attraction,*
         New York, Academic Press: 79-95.

Rosenblatt Paul C., and M. R. Cunningham

n.d.   "Sex differences in cross-cultural perspective," in B. B.
         Lloyd and J. Archer, eds., *Exploring Sex Differences,*
         London, Academic Press (in press).

Rosenblatt, Paul C., Stephen S. Fugita, and Kenneth V. McDowell

1969   "Wealth transfer and restrictions on sexual relations
         during betrothal," *Ethnology 8*: 319-28.

Rosenblatt, Paul C., Douglas A. Jackson, and R. Patricia Walsh

1972   "Coping with anger and aggression in mourning,"
         Omega 3: 271-84.

Rosenblatt, Paul C., and R. A. Phillips, Jr.

1975   "Family articles in popular magazines," *Family Co-
         ordinator 24*: 267-71.

Rosenblatt, Paul C., and M. G. Russell

1975   "The social psychology of potential problems in family
         vacation travel," *Family Coordinator 24*: 209-15.

Rosenblatt, Paul C., and D. Unangst

1974   "Marriage ceremonies: an exploratory cross-cultural
         study," *Journal of Comparative Family Studies 5*:
         41-56.

Sarnoff, Irving, and Philip G. Zimbardo

1961   "Anxiety, fear, and social affiliation," *Journal of
         Abnormal and Social Psychology 62*: 356-63.

Schachter, Stanley, and Jerome E. Singer

1962   "Cognitive, social, and physiological determinants of
         emotional state," *Psychological Review 69*: 379-99.

Schapera, Isaac

1938   *Handbook of Tswana law and custom*, London, Oxford University Press.

1940   *Married life in an African tribe*, London, Faber.

1950   "Kinship and marriage among the Tswana," in Alfred R. Radcliffe-Brown and C. Daryll Forde, eds., *African Systems of Kinship and Marriage*, London, Oxford University Press for the International African Institute: 140-65.

1953   "The Tswana," *Ethnographic Survey of Africa: Southern Africa, Part 3*, London, International African Institute.

Schebesta, Paul

1933   *Among Congo pigmies*, London, Hutchinson.

Scott, James G.

1882   *The Burman* (by Shway Yoe), 2 vols., London, Macmillan.

Seligman, Charles G., and Brenda Z. Seligman

1911   *The Veddas*, Cambridge, University Press.

1932   *Pagan tribes of the Nilotic Sudan*, London, George Routledge and Sons.

Silverman, P. R.

1972   "Widowhood and preventive intervention," *Family Coordinator 21*: 95-102.

Simmons, Leo W.

1945   *The role of the aged in primitive society*, New Haven, Yale University Press.

Smith, Mary F.

1954   *Baba of Karo: a woman of the Muslim Hausa*, London, Faber and Faber.

Smith, Michael G.

1955   "The economy of Hausa communities of Zaria," *Colonial Office Research Studies 16*: 1-264.

1965 "The Hausa of northern Nigeria," in James L. Gibbs Jr., ed., *Peoples of Africa*, New York, Holt, Rinehart and Winston: 121-55.

Souza, Gabriel Soares de

1851 "Tratado descriptivo do Brasil em 1587," *Instituto Histórico e Geográphico do Brazil, Revista 14*: 1-423.

Spier, Leslie

1930 "Klamath ethnography," *University of California Publications in American Archaeology and Ethnology 30*.

Spoehr, Alexander

1949 "Majuro; a village in the Marshall Islands," *Fieldiana: Anthropology 39*: 1-262.

Stair, John B.

1897 *Old Samoa*, London, Religious Tract Society.

Steward, Julian H.

1955 *Theory of culture change*, Urbana, University of Illinois Press.

Stirling, Matthew W.

1938 "Historical and ethnographical material on the Jivaro Indians," *U.S. Bureau of American Ethnology, Bulletin 117*.

Sugiura, Kenichi, and Harumi Befu

1962 "Kinship organization of the Saru Ainu," *Ethnology 1*: 287-98.

Swanson, Guy E.

1960 *The birth of the gods*, Ann Arbor, University of Michigan Press.

Thevet, André

1878 *Les singularitez de la France antarctique*, nouv. édition, Paul Gaffarel, ed., Paris, Maisonneuve (originally published in 1558).

1928   "Histoire d'André Thevet Angoumoisin, Cosmographe du Roy de deux voyages par luy fait aux Indes Australes et Occidentales," in Alfred Métraux, ed., *La Religion des Tupinamba*, Paris, Ernest Leroux: 239-52.

Tooker, Elisabeth

1964   "An ethnography of the Huron Indians, 1615-1649," *U.S. Bureau of American Ethnology, Bulletin 190.*

Townsend, P.

1963   *The family life of old people*, Baltimore, Penguin.

Toynbee, J. M. C.

1971   *Death and burial in the Roman world*, London, Thames and Hudson.

Tremearne, A. J. N.

1914   *The ban of the Bori*, London, Heath, Cranton and Ouseley.

Turnbull, Colin M.

1961   *The forest people*, New York, Simon and Schuster.

1965a   "The Mbuti pygmies of the Congo," in James L. Gibbs, Jr., ed., *Peoples of Africa*, New York, Holt, Rinehart and Winston: 281-317.

1965b   *Wayward servants*, Garden City, N.Y., Natural History Press.

Turner, George

1861   *Nineteen years in Polynesia*, London, Snow.

1884   *Samoa, a hundred years ago and long before*, London, Macmillan.

Tylor, Edward B.

1889   "On a method of investigating the development of institutions; applied to the laws of marriage and descent," *Anthropological Institute of Great Britain and Ireland, Journal 18*: 245-69 (reprinted in Frank W. Moore, ed., *Readings in Cross-Cultural Methodology*, New Haven, HRAF Press, 1966: 1-25).

Underhill, Ruth M.

1936   "The autobiography of a Papago woman," *American Anthropological Association, Memoir 46.*

1939   "Social organization of the Papago Indians," *Columbia University Contributions to Anthropology 30.*

1940   *The Papago Indians of Arizona and their relatives, the Pima,* Washington, D.C., U.S. Office of Indian Affairs.

1946   *Papago Indian religion,* New York, Columbia University Press.

Vernon, G. M.

1970   *Sociology of death,* New York, Ronald.

Voegelin, Erminie W.

1942   "Culture element distributions: XX Northeast California," *Anthropological Records 7*: 47-251.

Volkart, E. H., and S. T. Michael

1957   "Bereavement and mental health," in A. H. Leighton, J. A. Clausen, and R. N. Wilson, eds., *Explorations in Social Psychiatry,* New York, Basic Books: 281-307.

Vorren, Ørnulv, and Ernst Manker

1962   *Lapp life and customs; a survey* (Kathleen McFarlane, trans.), London, Oxford University Press.

Wallace, Ernest, and E. Adamson Hoebel

1952   *The Comanches: lords of the South Plains,* Norman, University of Oklahoma Press.

Walster, G. William, and T. Anne Cleary

1970   "A proposal for a new editorial policy in the social sciences." *American Statistician 24, no. 2*: 16-19.

Warner, W. Lloyd

1958   *A black civilization,* rev. ed., New York Harper and Brothers.

1961   *The family of God*, New Haven, Yale University Press.

Westermann, Diedrich

1912   *The Shilluk people: their language and folklore*, Philadelphia, Board of Foreign Missions, United Presbyterian Church of North America.

Whitaker, Ian R.

1955   *Social relations in a nomadic Lappish community*, Oslo, Norsk Folkemuseum.

White, Leslie A.

1959   *The evolution of culture*, New York, McGraw-Hill.

Whiting, Beatrice, and Carolyn Pope Edwards

1973   "A cross-cultural analysis of sex differences in the behavior of children aged three through 11," *Journal of Social Psychology 91*: 171-88.

Whiting, John W. M.

1968   "Methods and problems in cross-cultural research," in Gardner Lindzey and E. Aronson, eds., *Handbook of Social Psychology*, 2d ed., *vol. 2, Research Methods*, Reading, Mass., Addison-Wesley: 693-728.

Wiener, A.

1972   "The use of psychopharmacologic agents in the management of the bereaved," *Journal of Thanatology 2*: 799-806.

Williams, Francis E.

1930   *Orokaiva society*, London, Oxford University Press.

Winch, Robert F., and Donald T. Campbell

1969   "Proof? No! Evidence? Yes! The significance of tests of significance," *American Sociologist 4*: 140-43.

Wolf, Arthur P.

1970   "Chinese kinship and mourning dress," in Maurice Freedman, ed., *Family and Kinship in Chinese Society*, Stanford, Stanford University Press: 189-207.

Wretmark, G.

    1959   "A study in grief reactions," *Acta Psychiatrica et Neurologica Scandinavica, Supplement 136, 34*: 292-99.

Yamamoto, Joe, Keigo Okonogi, Tetsuga Iwasaki, and Saburo Yoshimura

    1969   "Mourning in Japan," *American Journal of Psychiatry 125*: 1660-65.

Young, E.

    1907   *The kingdom of the yellow robe*, London, Constable.

Indexes

Index of Names

Subject Index

58736